FROM A SHTETL TO THE WORLD

The Journey of an International Entrepreneur

Dr. Sinclair Rimmon

Editing by Brookes Nohlgren and
her exceptional team at Books By Brookes

Cover Design by Joseph Rubin

Printed in the United States of America

ISBN (Print): 978-0-9974513-7-5
ISBN (Ebook): 978-0-9974513-6-8

Library of Congress Control Number: 2016946686

Dedication

I dedicate this book to my wife, Joan; our children, Elana, Ron, Adina, Dan, and Alissa; their spouses, Scott, Dina, Angie, and Kenny; our grandchildren (from oldest to youngest), Simone, Dahlia and her husband, Danny, Gabriel, Kayla, Nava, Tamar, Annie, Ziva, Oren, Anat, Rachel, and Kate; my dear sister, Chana; all my family and friends; and the memories of my very dear parents, Yeshaiahu and Rachel, and my brother, Avraham.

Table of Contents

A Note from the Author

A WARM WELCOME to you, the reader of my book! In these pages, I will share my fascinating experiences, which include enduring poverty and hardship as a child in Warsaw; living for several years in a small Jewish village in Eastern Poland; moving to Palestine before the establishment of the State of Israel; working full-time while still a boy; rescuing refugees escaping to Palestine from war-torn Europe; fighting in Israel's War of Independence; traveling penniless to study at an American college; and working extremely hard to achieve my goals of becoming an international entrepreneur and a teacher. I have also realized the highest of all my dreams, to have a loving family.

I would like to explain a few aspects of this book, to help you as you read. First, you will find that I have been known by several different names throughout my life. When I was born in Poland, my parents gave me the Hebrew name Shmuel; this name also appeared on my documents in Israel. (An interesting note is that on some of my emigration papers, my name was written Szmul, with Sz representing the "sh" sound in Polish.) My friends in both Poland and Israel called me by the nickname Shami. In the United States, my school records and government documents referred to me as Samuel. (Samuel is the English equivalent of Shmuel.) When I became an American citizen in 1959, I took the first name Sinclair, to honor my father, who had a great admiration for author Sinclair Lewis, and the middle name David, to honor my mother's brother and my favorite uncle, David Duksin.

In Poland, our family name was Rymen. When we emigrated to the British Mandate of Palestine in 1934, however, my father wanted a name that sounded more Hebrew. He changed Rymen to the similar-sounding Rimmon, the Hebrew word for "pomegranate."

Throughout my account, I use some specialized terms as well as words from other languages, including Polish, Yiddish, and Hebrew. In each instance, a brief explanation accompanies the term, often in parentheses. A glossary at the back of the book includes the same words and provides fuller definitions for some.

On reflection, I feel a deep sense of gratitude to God for having blessed me and allowed me to survive the struggles of the early part of my life. This gratitude has motivated me to write a memoir of my personal experiences. I fervently hope that my life's story will inspire you to make your contribution to society.

Prologue

ON THE HOT MORNING of August 20, 2011, I was sitting with my wife, Joan, on the aft veranda of the luxurious Regent Seven Seas Mariner cruise ship. We were enjoying a delicious buffet breakfast and taking in the beautiful view. In the distance, I saw the magnificent, forested slopes of Mount Carmel. Closer in were the terraced Baha'i Gardens, surrounding the golden-domed Shrine of the Báb, as well as the immense development of Haifa, the largest city in northern Israel.

As the ship docked, I recalled events from almost eighty years earlier. When I was twelve, my father decided to move our impoverished family from Warsaw to Palestine, to fulfill his Zionist dreams and to escape the impending aggression of the Nazis. For two days, we traveled by train to Constanta, Romania, on the Black Sea, where we boarded a very old ship that carried both cargo and passengers. During the long journey, we crowded into one small steerage cabin. When the vessel arrived in the ancient port city of Jaffa, little motorboats lined up alongside it, to accept us passengers as we climbed down a rope ladder to be ferried to shore.

How different it was to travel on a Mediterranean cruise ship, in a stateroom with a balcony on deck eight. As we disembarked, a town car was waiting to transport us to the home of my dear sister, Chana, and her family.

My story starts in Warsaw, before the voyage to Palestine and shortly after the First World War…

Chapter 1

Fallen Chestnuts: My Life Begins in Warsaw

LIFE WAS VERY DIFFICULT for me as a youngster in Warsaw. At times, I was hungry for days. I remember getting ready to go to school one morning when I was about seven. I went into the kitchen and asked my father for my breakfast. He looked down at me and shook his head. He said solemnly, "Shmuel, my son, I'm sorry, but I don't have anything to give you for breakfast."

Disappointed, I replied, "Aba, after school, I'll return for lunch."

He paused, and with a resonating sadness, explained, "I'm sorry, Shmuel, but I won't have any lunch for you either. However, I will have a surprise for you for dinner."

I left without eating and met my friend Moniek in the courtyard. He addressed me by my nickname. "Shami, come join me. My mom gave me ten groschen. Let's go to the little grocery store." (Groschen was the currency in Poland.)

The grocery store was within the square of the courtyard, so the walk was very short. It was a modest little place, probably no bigger than a mini-mart you might see today. It had an assortment of basic goods like fruits and vegetables, dairy products, breads, and sweets. The items were crudely arranged in simple boxes. As we entered, the unmistakable aroma from the pickle barrel, which was immediately on the left, made me even hungrier.

Moniek picked up a kaiser roll and a pickle, and paid. As we walked out of the store together, he started eating, but he didn't offer me anything. Although I was very hungry, I was too embarrassed to ask for a bite of his food. I excused myself and told him I needed to go to the bathroom. I walked through to an empty corridor of the building, and there, when I knew I was alone, erupted into a flood of tears. I cried from hunger, shame, sadness, and my own helplessness. When my tears subsided, I continued on my way to the public school, where I studied in the morning.

In the afternoon, I attended the Tarbut school, where the curriculum was Hebrew studies. When school was over, I was famished, so I rushed home to see the surprise my father had for me. I found him in the kitchen. On the table was some bread that was several days old and hard as a rock. He rubbed garlic and sprinkled salt on the crust with the care of a fine chef. He cracked the bread, and his face brightened.

"I promised that you would have a treat tonight. Look what you are going to eat now. Smell it. This is salami!"

He served me the bread and poured me a glass of tea. Still beaming with excitement, he exclaimed, "You see, this is something that even rich people like to eat, salami and tea!"

I crunched through that hard bread as if it were the most delicious meal ever, and to this day, I still prefer hard bread. But now I eat it with a real slice of salami.

With my mother, Rachel; my brother, Avraham (in glasses); and my father, Yeshaiahu

I WAS BORN SHMUEL RYMEN in Warsaw on December 24, 1922, or the 5TH of Tevet, 5683, in the Jewish calendar

Warsaw was the capital of the resurrected Polish state in 1919. Before World War II, over 30 percent of Warsaw's population was Jewish. In fact, Warsaw had the second largest Jewish citizenry in the world, second only to New York City. It was a major center of Jewish life and culture in Poland, with many Jewish schools and synagogues.

My family consisted of my parents, Yeshaiahu and Rachel Duksin Rymen; my older brother, Avraham; and later my younger sister, Chana. We called our father *Aba* and our mother Ema, which are the Hebrew words for "father" and "mother." We lived on Nalewki Street, the busiest street in the Jewish community. Small factories and stores lined the

With my sister, Chana (middle); and my brother, Avraham (far right)

street-front, and large, four-story walk-up apartments stood behind them. While the factories and stores were mostly Jewish-owned, the apartment buildings were owned by gentiles.

Each apartment building had a courtyard paved in cobblestones. A gate at the courtyard's entrance was guarded by a gatekeeper. He closed the gate at midnight, and one had to pay him twenty groschen to gain entrance after that time. There were sidewalks in front of the stores, and tracks for the trolley cars down the middle of the street. At the end of the street was an open-air market with food vendors.

My mother was one of sixteen children born to Moshe and Sarah Duksin in the shtetl of Zhabinka, Poland, now in Belarus. (A shtetl was a small, largely Jewish village.) Zhabinka was first mentioned in Russian official papers in 1817. In 1882, a railway station was

My maternal grandparents, Sarah Starishevska and Moshe Duksin

built in Zhabinka on the line that connected Warsaw, Brest, and Moscow. (Zhabinka was 15 miles/25 kilometers northeast of Brest, and 145 miles/234 kilometers east of Warsaw.) Being on the railroad gave a powerful impetus to the development of the shtetl.

My father was one of six children born to Yoel and Hannah Shifrah Rymen in Kamenetz-Litovsk, Poland, now in Belarus. All I know about my grandfather is that he was a winemaker. He was known as Yoel der Viner, "Yoel the Winemaker."

Kamenetz was sixteen miles (twenty-six kilometers) north of Zhabinka. There was no train through Kamenetz, so residents had to travel to Zhabinka to catch the train to Warsaw, Brest, or Moscow. I never visited or met my family in Kamenetz.

My father, who was a very educated man, wanted to increase the range of his opportunities and felt that Warsaw would be a good place to achieve that goal. After my parents married, they left Zhabinka and settled in Warsaw. There, my father worked at the main Jewish newspaper, Haynt, which means "today" in Yiddish. After some time, he became an editor of the paper.

My mother was a very handsome woman who had learned how to sew. An active person, she opened a small general merchandise store (like a dime store of yore) and put her sewing skills to work by making foundation garments for women. My mother had a great fondness for particular movie actors, from both France and Germany. Her favorite was Maurice Chevalier, a famous French singer and actor. Occasionally, I would hear her singing his songs. One I remember is "Valentine."

My brother, Avraham, was born in January 1921. A beautiful child, he had light brown hair. My mother dreamed that Avraham would become a poet or an actor. I was born almost two years later, in December 1922, as I mentioned earlier. My sister, Chana, was born in September 1928. She was a sweet child, and everyone loved being around her. For as long as I can remember, she was always well-received and popular.

My paternal grandfather, Yoel Rymen

My father had cousins in Warsaw, the Rosenberg family, whom we visited quite

Left: With my brother, Avraham (right), ages three and four.
Right: My sister, Chana, age one

often on Shabbat, the Jewish Sabbath (day of rest and religious observance). Their son, Michel Rosenberg, went on to become well-known in the entertainment world. I will tell you more about him later.

During the Great Depression, business was not good enough to keep my mother's little store open, so she worked from home, and the newspaper did not pay my father regularly. In fact, for eleven months, he did not receive a regular paycheck. But he was loyal to the paper and continued working because he didn't want to lose his job.

Life was very difficult for us. The walk from our home to the public school I attended for the first half of the day was long. We were taught Polish literature, mathematics, geography, and history. My school was across the street from a large park, where I played with my friends and gathered chestnuts that fell from the trees. I enjoyed eating those chestnuts, especially on the days that I went without breakfast and lunch.

Like me, most of the children at school were from very poor families. One day when I was about eight, the principal announced that one student from each class would be chosen to attend a summer camp for two weeks. This camp would provide good food and pleasant activities. The children would be selected by a doctor who would come to the school to determine which youngsters needed it the most. We were all quite excited about the prospect and planned to reduce the small amount we ate even further, so we would be the skinniest and get chosen.

I was called in for my examination and asked to undress. I did as requested and stood before the doctor. He listened to my heart, weighed me, and measured my height. While I was still undressed, he said, "Son, you look pretty skinny. However, I still have other children to examine."

Encouraged by his words and convinced that I might be thin enough to win, I dressed and returned to class. A short time after the examinations were completed, the principal visited our class to inform us of the results.

"The doctor has completed the examinations. And the student from this class who has been chosen to go to camp is . . . Janek."

After the announcement, we all turned to look at him. There was not much life in Janek. In fact, he looked like a ghost. He was incredibly emaciated, with barely enough flesh to cover his bones; it looked like you could tear right through his white, paper-thin skin. When he heard his name, Janek tried to stand up to thank the principal, but he was so weak that he couldn't hold himself upright. I was greatly disappointed that I wasn't chosen to go to camp, and throughout my years in Warsaw, I never had an opportunity to do so. It wasn't until I became a camp counselor while in college in Los Angeles that I got to experience what a camp was like.

My family's circumstances grew increasingly difficult because of the depression in Warsaw, and I wanted to help out in any way I could. On the first day of our school vacation in early June, my friend D'vora and I stood anxiously in line in front of a ladies' hat factory, holding job applications. We were only eight, but D'vora's mother told us that the factory was looking for children because their small fingers were perfect for making the little artificial flowers that were put on hats. I had done similar work before, making holders for the lulavim (ritual palm fronds) used during Sukkot (the Feast of Tabernacles). Fortunately, we both got hired. The factory was on Nalewki Street, not far from where I lived.

The next day, we began making flowers for the ladies' hats of Warsaw. Our day lasted from eight in the morning until five in the early evening, with a short break for lunch, which was supplied by the company. It consisted of a slice of rye bread with butter, a tomato, a pickle, and a glass of water. Occasionally, we also got a little slice of herring. I was very happy to have that lunch, because there were many days that I went to work without breakfast.

Chapter 2

Black Cherries: Life in the Shtetl

EVEN THOUGH I CONTRIBUTED to my family's finances by working, circumstances in Warsaw grew more and more difficult. When I was almost nine, my parents told me they thought it would be best to send my sister and me to live with our maternal grandparents in Zhabinka. Food was more available in the shtetl, living conditions were more pleasant, and the extended family would offer support. In the summer of 1931, my mother, father, Chana, and I boarded a bus (the only mode of transportation we could afford) for the long journey to Zhabinka, which was 145 miles (234 kilometers) east of Warsaw. Avraham, who was ten, did not go with us, because he was attending a special school in Warsaw.

The roads were unpaved, and crude by modern standards. They had been built using nothing more than shovels and the strength of the men who wielded them. Constructed without machinery, they were full of rises and falls, bumps and pits. The wheels of the bus jolted over the rugged surface; the ride was roughest for those of us sitting at the back. The bus, which was already crowded, continued to make stops in small towns. With each additional passenger, the ride grew increasingly unbearable. Smoke mixed with sweat to create a noxious odor that made me want to throw up. I couldn't wait to get off!

When we finally arrived in Zhabinka, my grandparents greeted us with hugs and kisses. They were especially excited to see us because we had never met before! I felt overwhelmed with joy to be in that rustic area, away from the clamor of the city.

While my sister and I were thrilled to be in the country, *Aba* and *Ema* didn't share our enthusiasm. When it came time for them to get back on the bus, I also started to feel sad, realizing that they were really returning to Warsaw without us. My mother gave me a warm embrace and a big kiss before stepping onto the bus. My father, sensing my grief, kneeled and said, "Shmuel, my son, everything is going to be okay. You will have a good time here. You have lots of cousins to play with, and many family members to take care of you. It will be fun."

Tears welled up in my eyes and then trickled down my cheeks, but I continued to look at him and listen to every word.

My sister, Chana, age three

"You will live with your grandparents, and Chana will live with your aunt Esther. Please visit your little sister often and look out for her. Can you do that for me?" Chana was no more than three at the time.

I nodded and gave him a huge hug. Then he boarded

the bus and sat down next to my mother in the back. As they rode off, I could see them waving until they were out of sight. I would keep my word, checking on my sister as often as I could.

Zhabinka consisted of about two hundred families, the majority of which were Jewish. A few non-Jewish farmers lived on the outskirts. Zhabinka was a rural village, surrounded by wheat and dairy farms; in addition to cows, many other domestic animals were raised. My grandparents had sixteen children; some had died as infants, but most grew up and stayed in Zhabinka to raise their families. My relatives made up almost half the town's Jewish population!

These family members owned many of the little stores in Zhabinka and held vital positions in the community. My grandfather was the mohel (ritual circumciser), mashgiach (supervisor of kosher foods), and assistant to the rabbi. My mother's sister Esther owned the only bakery in Zhabinka. Aunt Hinde had a small grocery store, where she sold pickles, herring, cheese, and other dairy products. Uncle Yaakov also had a grocery store, where he sold nuts, candy, cereal, bags of wheat, and vodka. Uncle Abraham, who was my father's brother and Aunt Hinde's husband, owned a hardware store. My grandmother's brother, Moshe Starishevsky, had a fabric and clothing store.

Zhabinka's rabbi was the head of the community, chief official of the synagogue, cantor (person who sings liturgical music and leads prayer in Jewish services), and judge. He was responsible for resolving all disputes. When a legal disagreement was settled, the losing party had to pay him judicial fees. He earned his income this way.

Every Jew in the shtetl observed the traditions associated with holidays and family celebrations. As far as daily life in Zhabinka, there were no cars, buses, or even bikes. People got around by train or horse cart (or foot, of course). There were no radios, movie theaters, bars, or other sources of entertainment. Life basically centered on the family—education for the children, and work for the adults. Youngsters attended public school from eight in the morning until noon. We returned home for lunch and then attended cheder (a place of Jewish education) from three to seven. At cheder, we studied Hebrew, the Bible, and the Talmud (a text consisting of rabbinical discussions and interpretations of the Bible and Jewish law).

During my two-and-a-half years in Zhabinka, I lived with my grandparents in their small house. It consisted of a modest living room, which also served as a study and as a bedroom where all of us slept; a kitchen; and a tiny porch, where relatives and neighbors were entertained. The toilet was an outhouse in the backyard. In the winter, you might have to walk through five feet of snow to get to it!

The backyard also included a vegetable garden; a small barn housing a cow, which provided the milk for our homemade butter; a few chickens that roamed freely and supplied us with eggs; and a black cherry tree, which was my special joy. I had never seen a cherry, let alone a cherry tree, in Warsaw. I was fascinated by the tree's beauty—its gray, broken bark; long, shiny green leaves; and clusters of ripe, deep red fruit. I would often climb the tree and pick the delicious cherries. Sometimes I would eat so many that I would return to the house with a stomachache.

Most of the Jewish people in Zhabinka had similar homes, which, like ours, were located on the main street. The main street was about a mile from the train station. Several side streets led to public facilities, such as the synagogue and the mikvah (ritual bath). Those streets continued to neighboring Gentile (non-Jewish) farms, which were large estates with acres of orchards.

The summers were very pleasant in Zhabinka, particularly for us children. We attended cheder until the early afternoon, but for the rest of the day, until nine or ten in the evening, we played games. Sometimes, my older cousins took me to the Mukhavets River for a swim. Along the way, we passed through wheat fields where the stalks reached over our heads. The river was a meeting place for the area's teenagers, including the Gentiles.

My best friend in the shtetl was my cousin David Rymen, who was a few years older than I. Short and stocky, he had muscles upon muscles. David taught me how to play soccer during my first summer in Zhabinka. Our ball was improvised, made of pressed paper and tied together with string. David had a girlfriend, who lived on a distant farm. He communicated with her through homing pigeons, which he raised. One summer day, on Shabbat, he approached me early in the morning.

"Shami, I am going to visit my girlfriend today. Would you like to come with me? The trip will be long, but I think it would be good for you. You told me you had a little sweetheart in Warsaw." He meant D'vora, who had worked with me at the hat factory. "Since you are starting to keep company with girls, you should learn what you can from me about such affairs."

I agreed. I was always happy to join my cousin on his adventures, because they were typically filled with schticks (pranks) and games. We set out later that afternoon. Our journey began with a lengthy walk to the river. There, we climbed on a raft to continue to the farm. For most of the ride, David advised me about women. "It always takes a big effort to get to meet a girl and cultivate a relationship so she becomes your girlfriend. But you'll find out that it's always worth it." I wasn't quite sure what he meant, so I just listened and nodded.

We arrived at the farm at dusk and moved unnoticed to the barn. David boosted me up on a pile of hay to sleep while he met his girlfriend. "Maybe I'll introduce you to her in the morning, so you can see how gorgeous she is!" He roughed up my hair and scampered away. Exhausted from the long trip, I promptly nodded off.

I was asleep when David and his darling entered the barn and cuddled up somewhere down below me. I was awakened the next morning, just before dawn, by the sound of yelling. Her father had noticed she was missing and was calling for her. David jumped up and grabbed me, and we started running back to the river. I didn't even get to see her! My grandfather never knew about our exploit, because sometimes I would stay the night at David's.

I also spent time with my older cousins, Rifka and Aviva, ages eighteen and sixteen, respectively, who were daughters of my aunt Esther. On one occasion, Aviva invited me to the river, where she was meeting some girlfriends and some young men. As we walked to the river, we had time to talk. Like David, Aviva wanted to give me advice on relationships and growing up.

"When you get a little older, you will meet girls that you like. They will be interested in you, too, because you are quite good-looking. If you want to have fun with them and good relationships, you have to be kind and considerate."

When everyone arrived at the river, Aviva politely introduced me to her friends. I kept her advice in mind, and we all had a very pleasant time.

In the spring and summer, Sunday was always special because it was market day. Almost everyone would get up at six in the morning so as not to miss a minute of the excitement and amusement. Neighboring farmers transported their wares to the main street, which was filled with their horse carts. They brought sacks of wheat and barley, cows, sheep, ducks, chickens, and geese, as well as assorted fruits, nuts, and vegetables. The gathering was tumultuous. The sounds of clucking chickens, bleating sheep, and mooing cows mixed with the haggling and heckling of sellers and buyers. Occasionally, animals would escape and had to be pursued. It was quite a spectacle! By the late afternoon, just about all of the produce and livestock had been sold.

Many of the farmers used a good part of their earnings to buy implements from Uncle Abraham's hardware store, herring from the salty brine vats at Aunt Hinde's grocery store, white bread and challah (egg bread) from Aunt Esther's bakery, and vodka from Uncle Yaakov's store. The farmers relished this feast, sitting on their carts or on the ground, eating and drinking—and quickly becoming intoxicated. Eventually, they would all make it back to their farms safely and happily. We would return home happy, too, with the chickens and ducks we had bought, exhausted from the long day but in high spirits.

The winters in Zhabinka were very rough. The temperature might be as low as 20 degrees Fahrenheit (–7 degrees Celsius) for days or even weeks at a time. But the frigid weather didn't stop us from having fun. David and I would go to the river and glide on the ice, even though we didn't have skates. On occasion, other boys would join us, and we would have contests to see who could pee the farthest in the snow. The winner received a piece of chocolate from Aunt Hinde's store. (Aunt Hinde was David's mother.)

The snow was often up to our necks, and sometimes even higher! We trekked each day in the late afternoon to cheder, which was held in a room in the synagogue building. When we arrived, the melamed (teacher) greeted us. We would sit around a large table on wooden benches for our studies. The melamed used a conchik (thin leather strap) to subdue any child who dared to be rowdy, or to rouse one who fell asleep. We were more likely to receive lashes for falling asleep, because lessons in the freezing room were frequently dull, and we were tired from a full day of instruction at the public school.

I was rewarded for enduring those hours of learning. On Shabbat afternoons, my grandfather would test me on a page of the Talmud. (During this questioning, I occasionally sat on a sore bottom, compliments of the melamed.) If I passed the test, my grandfather gave me a ponchke (jelly doughnut), a delicacy from my aunt's bakery.

One Saturday, before administering the weekly questions, my grandfather sat me down for a talk. "Shmuel, you have been here for several months. You have visited all of your relatives, and you have seen all of Zhabinka.

Tell me, my grandson, do you feel better here than you did in Warsaw? Do you like school and cheder? Do you miss your parents terribly?" I was surprised by his inquiries, because we didn't have many conversations. My grandfather was quite a disciplinarian, and it wasn't like him to talk about feelings.

I told him, "Warsaw is a very interesting and lively city, but my life there was tough. I went hungry at times. I felt like I had to work, to make a contribution to our family's finances. I prefer the peaceful shtetl. I can just be a kid here! I miss *Aba* and *Ema* very much, but you and grandmother are very kind to me. I like school, but the melamed is not very nice sometimes. He uses his conchik too much."

My grandfather smiled, put his hand on my shoulder, and said, "Well, my melamed used the conchik on me a lot, too." I was surprised by my grandfather's words. Since he was so strict, it never occurred to me that he was once a boy who, like me, experienced punishment for disrupting the teacher's lessons or dozing off. I had always felt a warmth for my grandmother, and my grandfather's revelation made me feel very close to him, too.

Shabbat was a deeply special observance in Zhabinka. It started on Friday afternoon, when all the stores would close early except for my aunt Esther's bakery. Religious Jews do not cook on Saturday. In order to have a hot meal on the Sabbath, a dish called cholent was invented. This stew of beans, meat, and potatoes cooks slowly overnight. Every family would bring their pot of cholent to cook in the large oven in my aunt's bakery. The thought of the aroma of the cooking cholent still makes me salivate.

Most people, including children, rushed to the mikvah to cleanse themselves for the holy day. Later, my grandfather, as well as the rabbi and the rest of the synagogue leadership, would dress in a long, sashed black coat called a *kapote* and a fur hat called a *shtreimel*. Everyone else put on their fine Shabbat clothes, and all the males walked to the synagogue for the evening service. Afterward, my grandfather and I walked home for dinner. In the winter, after dinner, I would slog through the heavy snow to Aunt Esther's bakery. There, I slept on a platform above the warm oven, surrounded by the pots of cholent. Comforted by the sweet fragrances of the simmering stew, I dreamt of the coming Shabbat feast.

During every Jewish holiday, Zhabinka was in full celebration. Every Jewish-owned store was closed, and every man, woman, and child wore new clothes. Traditions were observed in both the synagogue and the home. My favorite holidays were Purim and Passover; I loved the joy and warmth associated with those occasions. Rosh Hashanah (Jewish New Year) and Yom Kippur (Day of Atonement) were more solemn, and observed very strictly. Everyone, including children over thirteen years old, fasted and prayed on Yom Kippur. Fasting was not difficult for me, because in Warsaw, I had to go without food from time to time.

School was closed for Purim. One year, I was chosen, with another child, to carry the *mishloach manot* (holiday gift basket of foods) that the richest family in Zhabinka had provided. The basket contained an apple, a pear, cookies, candy, and nuts; on top of these goodies was a Jaffa orange. The Jaffa orange was the most valuable of the items, because it had traveled all the way from *Eretz Yisrael* (Hebrew for "Land of Israel"). Our task was to carry the woven container filled with treats from house to house, to all the Jewish families in Zhabinka. At each home, the people inside got to look at the basket of food and smell it, but not touch it.

After making all our stops, we returned to the synagogue, where the rabbi received the *mishloach manot* in time for the reading of the book of Esther in the afternoon. Following his sermon, the rabbi opened the gift basket and distributed its contents to the congregation, with the children receiving their portions last. The rabbi peeled the precious orange with incredible care and gave a slice to each of his most loyal followers. When he called the youngsters, including me, each one of us got a piece of the peel. I smelled it and then ate it. That was my first and only taste of an orange until I went to Palestine in 1934.

As I mentioned, in addition to Purim, I also especially enjoyed Passover. Almost all of us got to wear something new for the holiday; my grandmother would give me a new shirt. School was closed for the entire eight-day festival. The spring air was still cold, and occasional rain turned the main street to mud, but there was no snow! The observation of Passover required a lot of preparation. My aunt Esther was particularly busy. Her bakery provided the matzah (unleavened bread) for every Jewish family in Zhabinka. But before the matzah could be made, any traces of chametz (leavened bread or cake, forbidden for use during Passover) had to be removed from the bakery. This meticulous cleaning took several days. When Aunt Esther invited Chana and me to help her make the matzah, we had to wash thoroughly before we were allowed into the bakery.

Passover included two seders (ritual meals), on the first and second evenings of the holiday. These seders included the telling of the story of the Jews' Exodus from Egypt in biblical times. One seder took place at my grandparents' house, where many of my relatives joined us. The family gathered at my aunt Esther's house for the other seder. At my grandparents' seder, I was given the special honor of reciting the *fier kashes.* These "four questions" are spoken at a specific point in the meal to illuminate why the night is special. At Aunt Esther's seder, my sister was chosen to recite. Each seder was observed very strictly, and we read the entire Haggadah (book of readings for the Passover seder). We also celebrated with joy and singing. To this day, Passover is still one of my favorite holidays.

Aside from religious holy days, life passed fairly simply in Zhabinka. There was one incident, however, that I recall strongly: I almost drowned in a pail of gasoline! In those days, like many children, I had head lice. The remedy at the time was dunking the entire head in a pail of gasoline. My uncle Pesach, my mother's youngest brother and only a teenager himself, implemented the treatment. He kept me under so long that I couldn't hold my breath anymore. I opened my mouth to breathe and started choking. Fortunately, my sister saw what was happening. She began shouting and crying, so Uncle Pesach pulled my head out of the pail.

I was so shaken that I shouted at my uncle, "What you did to me was very, very bad! I don't like you!" I was extremely angry at him, and the feelings lasted for a long

My family in Zhabinka, 1934

time. I turned to my sister and gave her a hug. We both ran away into the street. I told her, "I love you so much! What he did to me was terrible. Thank you so much for helping me." She looked at me, and without saying anything, grabbed me and hugged me back.

I had a warm and loving relationship with my little sister, which continues to this day. We often played together in the shtetl. Occasionally, she would tell me about Aunt Esther and her daughters. Aunt Esther embraced her as one of her own children, and my cousins loved her as if she were their own sister. I remember Chana had a radiant smile and a beautiful voice. She knew some Jewish songs, and when our family gathered, she would sing to all of us. I took great joy in her company.

My brother, Avraham, joined me at our grandparents' home in the summer. He would tell me about the private school he attended in Warsaw. An avid reader and a good writer, he brought books with him, a few of which contained poems. Avraham loved poetry. Now and then, he would recite poems to me—some original, and some from his books. I was not familiar with poetry, so I listened to the compositions with considerable attention. I liked the rhythm, imagery, and reflections on life that the words expressed. Because he was in Zhabinka for only a short while, we did not get to become very close friends. He was occupied with his own pursuits most of the time, but we were able to maintain a congenial relationship.

Avraham's visits aroused my interest in the humanities. Though still a boy, I knew that the education I desired was not available in Zhabinka. I would have to seek it elsewhere.

Chapter 3

Chocolate Ice Cream: A Sweet Farewell

ANTI-SEMITISM MADE LIFE DIFFICULT for Jews in Polish cities such as Warsaw, Vilna, Lublin, and Pinsk. Furthermore, the severe depression had left many Jews unemployed and impoverished. Therefore, at the time the Nazi Party was rising to power, some Jews from the larger Polish cities emigrated to Palestine, England, and South America. A very small number were allowed to enter the United States.

The brutal effects of the early Nazi movement were slower to reach the farm areas, where Jewish interactions with the Gentile population remained somewhat friendlier. Only occasionally would a Gentile with a big fruit farm send his dogs out to keep the Jewish boys from climbing the fences and picking his apples, pears, and plums. The dogs were quite ferocious, sometimes tearing our clothing and biting us. In fact, I was not fond of large dogs for a very long time. But overall, the Jews of the shtetl got along pretty well with their Gentile neighbors. Sadly, they did not, generally speaking, follow the movement of the Jewish population away from Central and Eastern Europe. As a result, most of them perished in the Holocaust.

Through his work at the newspaper, my father learned of the alarming conditions arising in Germany. An ardent Zionist (follower of the Jewish nationalism movement, which sought to reestablish a Jewish homeland in the historic Land of Israel), he wanted to move our family to Palestine. In 1934, my parents came to Zhabinka to bring my sister and me back to Warsaw. We traveled by horse-drawn cart to Brest-Litovsk, where we boarded a bus to the Polish capital.

On the trip back to Warsaw, I had very mixed feelings: I was pleased to be in the company of my mother and father again, but I had enjoyed life in the shtetl. My grandparents had been very kind to me, and my aunts and uncles had provided me with the spiritual and physical nourishment I lacked in Warsaw. I would miss my cousins, especially David Rymen; he had embraced me warmly and filled my days with exciting adventures. I was apprehensive about what daily life would be like now in my city of birth.

My friend Yadwiga Tratner, 1934

We stayed in Warsaw for several months, until we were able to relocate to Palestine. During that time, I again attended the public school. Because my parents were so busy arranging for our journey, I felt neglected and lonely. In my desolation, I reconnected with a friend, Yadwiga Tratner.

I had met Yadwiga at the public school before I went to Zhabinka. I often thought of her while I was away, and even missed her. To see her again and continue our friendship brought me joy. In my young eyes, Yadwiga was very beautiful and smart. She cheered and comforted me during the hectic period when we were selling my mother's inventory and making our travel plans.

Since I was not attending cheder then, Yadwiga and I spent many afternoons in the park across the street from the school. One of our favorite activities was gathering and roasting the chestnuts that lay scattered beneath the trees. We would also play with a ball that Yadwiga brought. Every now and then, we participated in volleyball games that took place in the park.

As we sat on the benches, Yadwiga would occasionally give me a hug and a kiss on the cheek. Heeding the relationship advice my cousins David and Aviva had given me in the shtetl, I treated her very kindly, listened to her and expressed an interest in her life, and sometimes gave her a hug and a kiss, too.

One day, I asked her if she was Jewish, and she told me she wasn't. But she didn't actually know *what* religion she was, since she didn't come from a religious family. I had felt uncomfortable being friends with a young lady who wasn't Jewish, so her lack of identification with a particular religion made me feel better. I tried to explain what being Jewish was all about. Surprisingly, she listened to everything I told her about the Five Books of Moses, which are known as the Torah and comprise the first five books of the Jewish Bible, and about keeping kosher (following Jewish dietary laws).

One afternoon, Yadwiga invited me home to meet her parents. They welcomed me very pleasantly when she introduced me as her dear friend from school. She gave me a tour of their apartment, which was not far from where I lived on Nalewki Street. But I was amazed at how big it was in comparison to ours! There were two bedrooms; a large living room with nice furnishings, paintings, and carpeting; and a large kitchen with an icebox, which was a large, non-electric, insulated cabinet with a chamber for holding large chunks of ice to keep food cold. Yadwiga's mother opened the icebox and produced some chocolate ice cream, which she served to us. I had never tasted this frozen treat before and was amazed at its wonderful taste and texture. I enjoyed every spoonful. Then we went out to a garden in the neighborhood and spent some more time talking about Judaism.

When I told Yadwiga I would be leaving Warsaw with my family, she started to cry and gave me a warm hug and a kiss. She said she wished she could go with me, but her parents wouldn't allow her to because she was their only child. We talked about writing to each other, but with the tumult of the move, we never exchanged any letters. I still remember Yadwiga as a very dear friend of my youth.

When our family was ready to go, we took our few belongings and traveled by train to Constanţa, Romania. There, we boarded a very old ship bound for Jaffa, the only port of entry into Palestine at the time. Sailing in steerage class, the five of us crowded into a small cabin on the lowest level of the boat. When the waters were rough, we suffered from mal de mer—seasickness. The food was poor. For breakfast, we were given an egg, bread or a roll, and coffee or tea. Lunch was similar, but fish replaced the egg, and a vegetable and salad (consisting mostly of lettuce) were added. Dinner closely resembled lunch. Happily, if someone had a birthday, a dessert was provided.

My sister and the other small children were served milk at all meals. Chana refused to drink it, however, so I had milk three times a day! Once, by a fortunate mistake, my brother and I were able to enjoy a second-class meal. We were standing near some children who were waiting for their parents on deck. The parents were late, so when the meal was served, we joined them. I don't remember what we ate, but it was our finest meal since leaving Warsaw!

Meanwhile, Chana won over the hearts of those around her, as she had also done on our long train ride to the port—and, before that, on our bus ride from Zhabinka back to Warsaw. She was always able to make friends and connect with others easily.

My most pleasant time during the voyage was when we were up on deck. Occasionally, the ship would pass through a narrow strait, and all the passengers, including us, would excitedly crowd the deck to get a glimpse of land on both sides. Because we had departed from a port on the Black Sea, we had to travel through the Bosporus Strait, a narrow and windy passage that divided Istanbul and connected to the Sea of Marmara.

Soon after, we passed through another strait, the Dardanelles, from the Sea of Marmara to the Mediterranean Sea—at least I thought it was the Mediterranean Sea! Looking at a map now, I realize that we first reached the Aegean Sea, and then the Mediterranean. As we navigated each strait, my father told me a little about the countries that we sailed by.

On one occasion, my father took me aside. He knelt down to my height and instructed me to look at the landmasses all around us. "Isn't it interesting, my son?" I stood speechless, waiting for his next words. "When you go to school in Palestine, you will eventually be required to take a course in geography. In it, you will learn a lot about different nations, seas, oceans, and other fascinating places." I never forgot my introduction to physical geography.

Later that evening, *Aba* explained more about why we were going to Palestine: He believed that a Jewish homeland should be reestablished there. *Ema* told us about her relatives who were already in Palestine. She said, "Children, I want you to know that my brothers are wonderful people, and you may learn a lot from them. They look forward to seeing all of us."

My uncle David Duksin, 1931

About two weeks later, we reached Jaffa. Small boats manned by Arabs came out to transport us to the shore. The men shouted in Arabic, "*Salam alaikum! Keef halak!*" None of us knew what the words meant, so we didn't respond. After arriving in Tel Aviv, we learned the meaning: "Peace be unto you! How are you?" I was pleasantly surprised by the warmth of their greeting.

We took a bus from Jaffa to Tel Aviv and then nineteen miles (thirty kilometers) further to the moshav Kfar Hess, where my mother's brother, David Duksin, owned a farm. A moshav is an Israeli cooperative community made up of small farms. We stayed for a few days with Uncle David while my father arranged for an apartment for us in Tel Aviv. There, we lived at 4 Shenkin, across the street from Shuk HaCarmel, which was and still is a very large and popular open-air marketplace.

At the time, I was anxious to improve my life, having learned from my experiences in Warsaw and Zhabinka. My immediate goals were to go to school, get a good job, make friends, and become a happy and successful teenager.

Chapter 4

Jaffa Oranges: A Young Pioneer in Palestine

WE BEGAN OUR LIFE IN TEL AVIV in the summer of 1934. My father found work as a city department head, at the municipal offices on Bialik Street. After two months, once again, my parents sent me and my sister to live with relatives who could provide a more comfortable existence. This time, we went to Petach Tikvah, a city seven miles (eleven kilometers) east of Tel Aviv, to stay with our cousin Hannah, the daughter of my father's brother, Abraham, and her husband, Aron Novodvorski. (Hannah was also the daughter of my mother's sister Hinde.) My brother remained with my parents in Tel Aviv to attend a special public school. *Aba* and *Ema* believed Avraham's potential would be cultivated there.

Thankfully, the bus ride from Tel Aviv to Petach Tikvah was much faster—and far less bumpy!—than the one from Warsaw to Zhabinka. Petach Tikvah was a small community, with eight to ten thousand residents. Much of the land surrounding the town was used for agriculture, in particular for growing citrus fruits, almonds, and grapes. The world-famous Jaffa orange was produced there and exported to Europe. Additional industries had developed as a result of the abundant citrus crops. Therefore, many people were employed in agriculture in some manner.

Our cousin Hannah met us at the station. Hannah and Aron owned a home. He worked as a fund-raiser for Jerusalem yeshivas (schools of higher Jewish learning) and traveled to different countries to collect the monies. He was quite successful and in a better financial situation than my parents. Hannah and Aron didn't have any children of their own at the time, so they were very happy to have us.

When we arrived at Hannah's house, she said, "I welcome you to my home as if you were my own children! I know you will miss your mother and father, but I hope I can make you comfortable so that you will enjoy your time here." Her words raised my spirits because, even though I was with my sister, being away from my parents and brother again was tough on my heart. She gave us both a hug and continued, "My husband is now in Europe working, but I will be here with you."

After we settled in, Hannah took us to a little market nearby to shop for vegetables. She introduced us to some of the people there, making the same announcement each time: "These are my cousins, Shmuel and Chana. Whenever you see them, please be nice to them!"

The outing took longer than expected, so my sister and I were both tired when we returned. Chana went off by herself to relax. My cousin, still beaming with warmth and energy, explained to me, "It is summer now, and soon I will try to enroll you in school. In the meantime, you can spend some time at home and get to know Petach Tikvah. You will also meet our uncle Noach!" Noach Duksin was my mother's brother.

During the first couple of weeks in Petach Tikvah, I spent a lot of time with my sister. We played soccer—but with a real ball instead of one made from pressed paper! We would also go for walks and explore the town. Together, we learned about our neighborhood. Eventually, we got to know some of the other children and began making friends.

We did meet our uncle Noach. He was a pioneer, having immigrated to Palestine in 1923 to join his brother David, who had arrived a few years earlier. He originally worked in the *pardes* (orange grove). Eventually, he became a supervisor of public works. His job was to extract water from the ground and move it to where it was needed. You would never have guessed he was the man in charge by watching him work, because he labored alongside his employees in every aspect of a project. He was a very attractive man—tall, muscular, and tan. On most of the occasions I saw him outside of work, he was accompanied by a lovely young woman. Sometimes, he would have one on each arm.

My maternal uncles David Duksin (left) and Noach Duksin (right), in the 1950s

Uncle Noach was always very kind to me and my sister, often hosting us at his home for meals. Occasionally, he asked me to visit him at his work site. I would find him deep inside an enormous hole in the earth, where he and his team were digging a well. On Saturdays, he would play poker with his friends; sometimes, he invited me to watch. He explained, "Someday, after you have learned all the rules, you will be able to play yourself." Many years later, when I started playing poker with my friends in B'nai B'rith (a Jewish service organization), I remembered what my uncle had taught me. I still enjoy the game.

After Uncle Noach and his friends finished playing cards, we would all have a treat—a meal featuring dark bread, sardines, and vegetables, with cake and tea for dessert. I learned a lot from the conversations after the games. The men would talk about Zionism, to which my father had already introduced me; problems in the town; issues with the Arab community; and, of course, women. The passion with which they engaged in these discussions, and the vigor with which they worked, reflected the deep commitment these pioneers had to building a real home for the Jewish people.

Later that summer, I went to work in a gasoline warehouse not far from my cousin's house. The warehouse served as a gas station and was situated on the busy main street, which was part of the primary route to and from Tel Aviv. My job was to carry heavy containers of gasoline and, using a funnel, to fill the gas tanks of the trucks. (Automated pumps did not exist at the time.) Lugging the heavy containers around was incredibly hard work, and the hours were long.

A young Arab boy named Makhmoud worked there with me. He spoke a little Hebrew, and I knew a little Arabic, so we were able to communicate adequately and work very well together. Some days, we would share our lunches. I often brought a can of sardines, and he brought green olives and pita bread. He was amazed when he first saw the sardines. I had eaten them my whole life, so they seemed ordinary to me; I couldn't understand why he was so interested in them!

One day, he pointed to the can, and in his best Hebrew (which was heavily mixed with Arabic), he said emphatically, "Shami, I would very much like to bring some sardines home to show my parents. Please! Please let me have some! And I will bring you some dates." He gestured to indicate how many of the little fish he wanted.

I didn't understand every word he said, but I got the message. In my best Arabic (mixed with Hebrew), I replied, "Makhmoud, how about this—I'll bring you an entire can of sardines tomorrow, and you can bring me some dates." He agreed with great enthusiasm and thanked me profusely. The transaction took place the next day. I tasted dates for the first time, and they were delicious! He said his parents enjoyed the sardines very much. The exchange with Makhmoud was my first win-win negotiation!

Whenever we got the chance to sit down and relax, we would talk about our families and our lives outside of work.

"You're lucky," he began. "You live in a big, beautiful city! I live in a small village a few kilometers from here." He paused. I wondered what he thought was so fortunate about my life. I had never considered myself lucky. Doing backbreaking work at twelve years old, when I really wanted to be going to school, did not seem lucky. I wanted to understand him better.

"What makes you think that?" I asked.

"Well," he said, "you live in a home with only your cousins and your sister. You get to have some room to yourself.

To me, that's lucky. I have seven brothers and sisters, and we all share two rooms." He explained that his family lived on land that was owned by an effendi, a wealthy Arab absentee landlord, who housed his workers in shacks. Their efforts went to enriching his wealth. "And," he continued, "my father labors in the fields and hardly makes any money. That's why I decided to work, so I could help him."

I couldn't imagine living in such a crowded space. In Warsaw and Zhabinka, our quarters were never so cramped—so perhaps I was luckier than I thought. Makhmoud worked to help take care of his family. I could relate to that experience, and hearing his story made me feel more connected to him. I remembered when my dad worked without pay in Warsaw, and we had no food at times. How I wished I could have helped my family more than I did, by working at the hat factory. I was grateful now always to have food on the table. Though my cousin was able to provide for my sister and me, I felt compelled to work and make a contribution.

Makhmoud and I grew to become good friends. In time, I learned a little more Arabic from him, and he learned a little more Hebrew from me. Sometimes, we would stay overnight at the warehouse when it closed late and we didn't feel like making the trip home. On those occasions, we would improvise beds by layering newspapers and any other paper we could find on the ground. As you can imagine, our "mattresses" were quite uncomfortable.

Coming home from work was always a treat. My sister would give me the biggest hug she could and relay all the stories my cousin had shared with her during the day. Just like my aunt Esther in Zhabinka, Hannah loved my sister and treated her as if she were her own child. To my delight, Chana would also sing the new songs my cousin had taught her. When I could, I would take my sister out to get Elite chocolates or ice cream. (Elite was a popular candy manufacturer, founded by a Russian Jew who had immigrated to Palestine.)

Hannah was a very good cook, but because I was usually working, I had few opportunities to enjoy her meals—except on Friday evenings. I always looked forward to Shabbat dinner, not only for the delicious food but for the loving company of my family. I would make the blessing over the wine, and my sister, with her sweet voice, would recite the blessing of the bread. I learned a great deal about my cousin from our conversations as we ate. I remembered Hannah from when we all lived in Zhabinka. At the time, she was already a young woman, so we didn't interact much. Still, I recalled that she was very warm and friendly, and quite attractive. I also remembered Aron. He owned a hardware store, where I occasionally stopped to browse. I certainly recalled that he was very enamored with Hannah!

One Sabbath eve, Hannah told us the story of how she arrived in Petach Tikvah. "I met Aron in Zhabinka when I was only sixteen," she began. "I enjoyed spending time with him, but I wasn't looking for a serious commitment. He wanted to marry me! I didn't know how to handle it, and he didn't stop pursuing. He was so insistent! I decided the best thing to do was to leave. That's when I went to stay with your parents in Warsaw, while you were with our family in Zhabinka.

"But he found me in Warsaw!" she continued. "And was still insistent on getting married! I wasn't ready for that, so I left again, this time traveling to Palestine to join Uncle Noach. Yet it wasn't long before Aron found me again! After so much persistence, I finally agreed to marry him, and I'm so glad I did. He is a fine man, and we have a very pleasant life together."

I found my cousin's account quite humorous. The idea of following a girl all over the place reminded me of my cousin David's quest to see his sweetheart on the farm. The things men did for love seemed to require more effort than sense!

During those dinners, Hannah would ask me about my job. She once said, "I'm not sure it's a good idea for you to work so hard, but I admire your commitment and effort." She added with a smile, "You're a very young chalutz!" Chalutz is the Hebrew word for "pioneer."

While I was working in the warehouse, Hannah would usually make me a sandwich, or give me a can of sardines and some vegetables. When I tried to offer her some of my earnings, she would close my hand around the money and say, "You work so hard for what you earn. It's yours. You should use it to buy something for yourself, like a new pair of shoes."

At the end of the summer, school began. While no arrangements were made for my sister to attend, my cousin had enrolled me. After going for a few weeks, however, I learned about employment opportunities in the orange groves. One of my friends explained, "We'll pick oranges, wrap them, and send them to Europe. We'll also get to meet other teenagers. It'll be fun! Plus, we'll earn some money."

I pondered the idea as I walked home that day. I was reminded of the Purim in Zhabinka when I had carried the gift basket with the Jaffa orange—and received a sliver of the peel from the rabbi. Now I imagined that I might have the chance to have an entire orange to myself! How exciting it would be to work surrounded by oranges! My enthusiasm grew, so when I arrived home, I approached my cousin with my plan.

"I would like very much to work in the orange groves with some of my friends," I said. "I can even make some money!"

"But what about school?" she asked.

"Don't worry! I'll take classes in the evening and work during the day. I'll do my best to attend school as often as possible."

"Well," she began with some reluctance, "you are twelve now, and if this is what you really want to do, I am not going to stand in your way."

Although I was young, I knew how important working was. I remembered our impoverished days in Warsaw. To me, the only way to avoid going hungry was to provide for myself by working, so that's what I chose to do. I took the job and started immediately.

My day began early. I awoke at 5:30 in the morning to start my long walk to the orange groves, which were several miles outside of Petach Tikvah. The more seasoned laborers rode donkeys to work. On occasion, one of them would see me walking and offer me a seat behind him. While I enjoyed the break from traveling on foot, I always had a hard time sitting down afterward! My task was to carry large, heavy baskets of oranges from the groves to the trucks, a distance of about thirty feet. I worked from 7:00 a.m. until 5:00 p.m. for a salary of ten prutot (coins with the value of one cent).

Although I enjoyed eating oranges every day during my lunch break, I decided that the job was too difficult for me. The hard work wasn't worth the pay. Thinking there had to be a better way to earn money, I chose to wrap oranges instead. (In order to preserve the oranges for their long journey to Europe, each one had to be enclosed in paper in a specific manner.) I requested and was granted a transfer to that area of the operation. After two evenings of instruction, I went to work. Wrapping oranges paid double what I was making before, and the job was significantly easier. I worked with about a dozen others, most of whom were younger men. I made friends with several who were close to my age.

Because I focused so much on working during my time in Petach Tikvah, I did not regularly attend school. Only when I returned to Tel Aviv two years later was I able to pursue my education.

Chapter 5

A Carp in the Bathtub: My Bar Mitzvah

ALTHOUGH I WAS BUSY WORKING, I still found time for my family. My uncle David (the brother of my mother and my uncle Noach) had invited me to spend some time with him on his farm in Kfar Hess, and I had accepted. Before I was to go, however, I received a letter from my parents saying that my bar mitzvah would take place in Tel Aviv the following Saturday, on my thirteenth birthday. Excitedly, I announced to all my relatives in Petach Tikvah that this meaningful event was to happen: "My parents have asked me to come to Tel Aviv! We are going to celebrate my bar mitzvah!" I invited my uncle Noach to join me. I also wrote to my uncle David to inform him of the good news, to request his presence at the occasion, and to explain that my visit would be delayed by a week.

Regrettably, my uncle Noach couldn't leave his work responsibilities. My uncle David also had to decline. Somewhat discouraged by their responses, I approached my cousin Hannah.

"Can you join us at lunch after the ceremony?" I asked her. "I would be honored if you would celebrate with me."

"My dear Shami, I would love to attend your bar mitzvah," she said. "But Aron will be arriving from Europe any day now. I want to be home to welcome him. I don't want him to return to an empty house. You understand, don't you?"

"I do," I replied. "Can my sister come with me?"

She paused before responding. By this time, she had become very attached to Chana and was hesitant to be separated from her. She replied, "Shami, you are growing into a young man, but your sister is still a little girl. I don't feel it would be safe for her to travel with you. That would be too much responsibility."

I understood Hannah's concerns but was saddened by her answer. Still, I knew I had to go to Tel Aviv no matter what. So the Thursday before my bar mitzvah, my cousin and my sister accompanied me to the bus station and saw me off.

When I arrived at my parents' apartment on Shenkin Street, I was warmly received by them and by my uncle Pesach, who was also living there. *Aba* and *Ema* were already making plans for Shabbat.

That night, my father began preparing me for the ceremony. We sat down together to practice the passages that he and I would have to recite. We would go to a minyan (prayer quorum) on Shabbat morning at the *shtiebel* (small chapel) in Tel Aviv's Great Synagogue, on Allenby Street. I would read a portion of the Torah. According to Jewish tradition, a boy of thirteen is considered an adult; therefore, he is responsible to take on all religious obligations. Before that time, the boy's parents are accountable for him. As part of the bar mitzvah ritual, the father publicly declares his release of that responsibility. At the proper time, he says, "*Baruch sh'petarani m'onsho shel zeh*" ("Blessed is the One who exempted me from the obligations of this son").

When I woke up Friday morning, my parents presented me with my bar mitzvah gift—a shiny new pair of black shoes! Until then, I had always worn secondhand shoes, so having my own new pair made me very happy. Wanting to make sure I was presentable for the ceremony, I went to take a shower. But I found that the tub was occupied—by an enormous carp, swimming about freely! My mother wanted the gefilte fish for the celebratory lunch to be as fresh as possible. Originally, gefilte fish was made by combining ground fish, spices, and finely chopped vegetables. This mixture was then stuffed into a whole carp. (*Gefilte* means "stuffed.") The stuffed fish was cooked in broth and then sliced to create servings of the stuffing surrounded by the carp steak. My mother's rendition of this Jewish delicacy was especially tasty. Nowadays, most people know gefilte fish only as the ground fish patties that come in a jar—not in a fish!

Saturday morning, I rose full of eagerness. I looked forward to participating in the ceremony and spending time with my family. Since women did not customarily attend the service, my mother stayed home to be ready for lunch. (The ceremony would be followed by a small meal, unlike the extravagant receptions with catered food and hundreds of guests that often occur today.) My uncle Pesach wasn't able to attend the service. I was disappointed that no one I invited could be there, but I was happy to have some time with my father.

The ceremony was a simple affair. My father and I entered the *shtiebel* and waited our turn to recite the designated passages in front of the worshipers. *Aba* knew some of the people, and some he didn't. I wasn't nervous, because the reading was quite similar to what we had practiced. When we finished, the rabbi offered some words of congratulations. And my bar mitzvah was over.

As my father and I returned home for lunch, I started settling into my new shoes. How comfortable they were! I noticed that our walk was quiet, signifying that something important had happened and this was a time to reflect on it. My father explained the moment to me.

"Shmuel, my son, I want you to know that today you are responsible for what you do and accomplish. I hope that you will live a good life."

I remained silent, listening to his words and pondering them. I had already been doing hard work for almost a year in Petach Tikvah—the kind that bronzed my uncle Noach's skin and sculpted his body into muscle. I knew what dedication looked like. I was wise with my earnings and saved as much as I could. I understood how important it was to be able to provide for oneself. I felt prepared to be an adult.

As we walked through the front door, my mother greeted me. She gave me a hug and a kiss and said, "Congratulations on becoming a bar mitzvah!" (The term *bar mitzvah* can be used to refer not only to the coming-of-age ceremony but to the young man himself.) My uncle Pesach, who had returned in time for lunch, also gave me his good wishes.

We all sat down to eat the gefilte fish my mother had prepared. After thanking my parents for lunch and for the new shoes, I told them about my invitation to stay with Uncle David for a few weeks.

My mother said, "My brother is a very good man, and you can learn a lot from him. I hope you will enjoy your time there."

I had been looking forward to socializing with my own brother, but I hadn't seen him since arriving. My parents told me he was visiting a friend's family. On the following Friday, he returned, and we had a short conversation. I learned that he was doing well in high school, where he had met many nice friends and teachers. He enjoyed his studies very much. He became especially animated when he spoke about poetry and literature. His enthusiasm rekindled my interest in going to school. I realized that I was missing the intellectual and social stimulation of a serious academic experience.

Later that day, I said goodbye to Avraham and to my uncle Pesach. I parted from my parents with hugs and kisses. Then I got on a bus to Kfar Hess, to visit my uncle David on his farm.

Chapter 6

Milk and Eggs: Working on My Uncle's Farm

A CURVY NINETEEN MILES (thirty kilometers) north of Tel Aviv, Kfar Hess bordered Arab land. When I arrived, there was no one to meet me at the station. I learned later that this was simply how things were done in Kfar Hess. The farms were off the main road, and somehow people made their way to and from the bus station. Uncertain where to go, and a bit disconcerted, I approached a bus driver at the terminal.

"Excuse me, sir," I began. "I'm here to visit my uncle. His name is David. He owns a farm here."

"David Duksin? Oh, yes! He's a very nice gentleman. I have driven him and his family to Tel Aviv several times."

He pointed me in the right direction and instructed me where to go. As I walked, I noticed that Kfar Hess was completely different from Petach Tikvah and Tel Aviv, which were more urban. There were other farms in the vicinity of my uncle's, and they all looked pretty much the same. When I arrived at what I thought was my uncle's farm, the cacophony of a mooing cow and clucking chickens greeted me. I was assured I was in the correct place when my uncle saw me and came out of his house. He welcomed me with a bear hug that made me think my bones might break! Then he slapped me on the back. David was just being affectionate, but because he worked so hard in the fields, he was exceptionally strong. I felt that slap for several days!

"I am very, very happy to see you!" he cried. The conversation continued as he invited me into the house. "You will live here as my own son during your stay. As you can see, my children are not home at the moment. They are with their mother, my wife, in Tel Aviv for a while. So for some time, it will be just you and me. We'll be sure to have a good time!"

I had arrived around lunchtime. My uncle offered me a glass of milk as we sat down for our meal, which consisted of several hard-boiled eggs and a piece of bread. As we ate, he shared a bit about himself. "Like my brother Noach, I am a chalutz. I left my family in Zhabinka because I was a Zionist and wanted to help build *Eretz Yisrael*, just like him." David went on, "I have this small farm, and it will be a good experience for you to help me in my work. I hope you will grow up to be a pioneer yourself!"

My uncle said he would treat me like his own son, and he kept his word: I was awakened the next morning before dawn. He burst into the room and announced, "It's time to milk the cow!" I stumbled to my feet and dressed, following him into the small barn. He handed me a large pail.

"What's this for?" I asked.

"Well, what else could it be for?" he said with a laugh. "It's for collecting the milk!"

Since I had clearly never milked a cow before, my uncle showed me how to squeeze the teats and aim into the pail so as not to spill any milk. On my first attempt, I shot milk directly in my face. On the second, milk went into my mouth and drenched my shirt. I still remember swallowing some and being surprised by how warm it was. Pleasantly, it reminded me of the fresh milk I drank in Zhabinka. Eventually, I learned the proper way to milk the cow and was able to do it on my own.

When that task was completed, we returned home for a hearty breakfast of vegetables, eggs, black olives, and bread with butter. We also had some hot tea. After a brief rest, my uncle said, "Now it's time to tend the garden. Then we will gather the eggs."

The entire farm wasn't very big, maybe two dunams (equal to just under half an acre). The house consisted of two bedrooms, a living room, and a kitchen, which had a small table and chairs for dining. The living room featured a little sofa and several chairs. The walls were decorated with pictures of Jewish leaders, including a large one of Theodor Herzl, the founder of modern political Zionism.

The farm was made up of a coop that housed almost a hundred chickens, a small shed for the cow, and an outhouse. The rest of the arable land was covered with an assortment of vegetables, including tomatoes, cucumbers, peas, and green beans. My uncle showed me how to spread fertilizer on the plants. The stench was quite strong. Later, we gathered the eggs from the chickens and put them in a basket. My uncle had cautioned, "Shmuel, be very careful when you pick up the eggs and especially when you place them in the basket. If one breaks, it makes a mess on the others, and we can't sell them. Let's do our best to avoid that." Indeed, I was very mindful to keep the eggs intact.

We brought the basket of eggs to a communal warehouse, where my uncle explained the farming business to me. "Shmuel," he said, "Kfar Hess is a moshav, a cooperative. I bring all the produce from my farm, along with any eggs and milk, to this warehouse. All the other farmers in Kfar Hess do the same. Then the grocers in charge arrange to transport the goods to Tel Aviv and sell them there. We earn a portion of the money when our goods are sold. You see, although we own our farms independently, we work together to market our produce. It's part of our mission to build Eretz Yisrael. We provide the food that feeds the city." I found this purpose of the moshav to be very inspiring.

I spent more time on the farm during my school vacations. Also, on some weekends, Uncle David invited my family from Tel Aviv for a visit. He would open his home to us and show us warm hospitality, sharing all the produce of his farm. Vegetables, milk, cheese, and eggs were expensive in Tel Aviv, and my parents, like many others, could not afford them.

My uncle and I shared a funny secret. Commercial fertilizer was rare and expensive, so most farmers used cow manure instead. But when relatives came to visit, their trips to the outhouse provided my uncle with a new source of fertilizer—and he claimed it was the best kind. So when the family commented on his fine fruits and vegetables, he would wink at me and smile, knowing that these same people had been responsible for enriching the soil that produced the lovely tomatoes and cucumbers they were eating.

These gatherings on my uncle's farm gave us the opportunity to share our experiences and discuss our challenges.

For example, I found out that the Arabs in the neighboring village sometimes shot their guns at night, which threatened and frightened the members of the moshav. This apparent act of aggression baffled me, because my relationship with Mahkmoud in Petach Tikvah was so pleasant.

I gained a lot from my visits with my uncle. I learned that every job requires specific training and carries its own responsibilities. I experienced the diligence and determination that lead to successful self-employment. I discovered that for a business to function and thrive, its components must be understood and coordinated. I witnessed the benefits, including joy, that come from working cooperatively and congenially with others in business. Mostly, I felt the fulfillment and satisfaction of being able to provide for one's family and friends. Above all else, I gained a kind uncle, who also grew to be a dear friend.

After staying in Kfar Hess for several weeks following my bar mitzvah, I returned to my cousins' home in Petach Tikvah and went back to working at the gasoline warehouse.

Chapter 7

Communal Meals: Laboring on a Kibbutz

IN THE SUMMER OF 1937, after a total of three years in Petach Tikvah, I finally returned to Tel Aviv to live with my parents. Chana arrived several weeks later and was received with great warmth. Speaking of Chana, I will share a bit about the coming years for her. As my sister grew up, her goal was to be a nurse. When she reached the appropriate age, she enrolled in a nursing program at the Hadassah hospital in Jerusalem. Graduates were offered the opportunity to be employed at the medical facilities. So when she completed her studies, she started working there; eventually, she advanced to the position of head operating room nurse.

Meanwhile, on October 21, 1937, just short of my fifteenth birthday, I started attending the Gymnasium Erev, a night school in Tel Aviv. Classes were held from 6:00 to 10:00 on weeknights. The students at the school shared the same hardships and aspirations I did, so making friends there was easy. One friend, David, used to walk with me to and from school. One night after class, we talked about our ambitions.

He said, "My parents are struggling financially, like yours and many others. I go to school at night so I can work

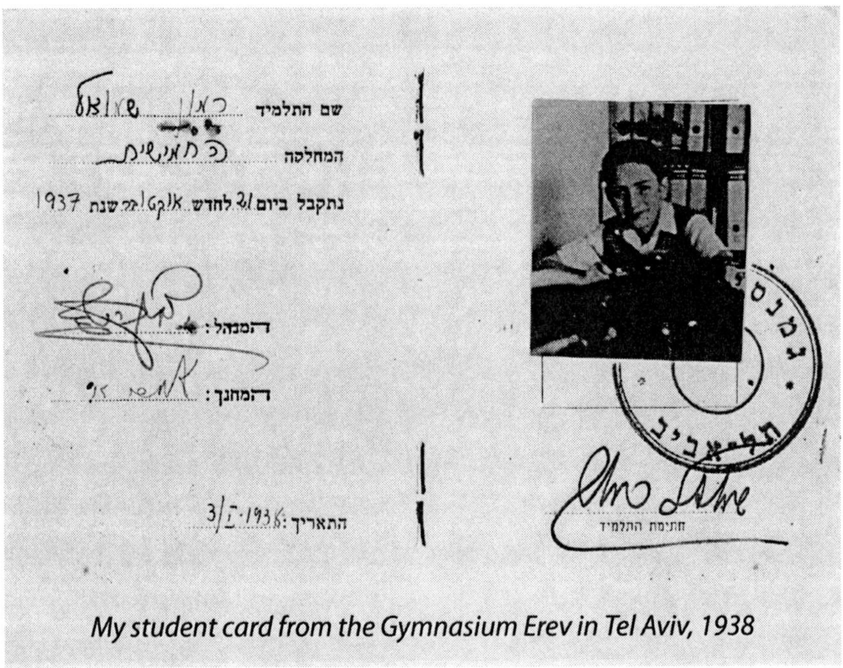

שם התלמיד

המחלקה

נתקבל ביום ... לחדש ... שנת 1937

המנהל:

המחנך:

התאריך:

חתימת התלמיד

My student card from the Gymnasium Erev in Tel Aviv, 1938

during the day to help them out. But I also want to save money to attend the Hebrew University. What are your plans?"

"My goals are the same as yours," I told him. "I want to help my parents, and I also want to attend the Hebrew University." We continued discussing our educational objectives, and before we parted, he said, "I hope we see each other at the university someday!" Our lives took us in different directions, but we occasionally met by chance and were so happy to share a short time together.

I was fortunate to secure a job making bike deliveries for Green Brothers, a firm that imported pharmaceuticals. I worked from 8:00 a.m. to 5:00 p.m., Monday through Friday, for a salary of ten lira (twenty-eight dollars) a month. I worked at Green Brothers for fourteen years, except for the time I spent in the military, until I left to go to the United States.

Although I was tired by the time evening came around, I enjoyed school very much. The teachers were empathetic to us students, recognizing that we all worked during the day. The school was owned and managed by an instructor in his forties who had a PhD from the Hebrew University of Jerusalem. He had established the school with several other teachers, acquiring a building with about half a dozen rooms for classes and receiving a license from the city of Tel Aviv. His aim was to provide education for youngsters who were employed.

While I liked all of the instructors at the school, my favorite was my geography teacher. A kind and friendly woman, she would always stay a few minutes after class to answer any questions I had about the lessons or about other countries. We eventually became friends. Impressed by my keen interest in geography, one day she asked me how it started.

With my friend David (right) in Tel Aviv, 1941

"My interest was first aroused when I traveled with my family from Warsaw to Jaffa," I explained. "Now I always enjoy hearing the stories of pioneers who arrived in Palestine from so many different places. I also have a small collection of stamps from around the world. The colorful images on the stamps piqued my curiosity about distant lands."

"But you haven't visited any of these places, have you? How do you get the stamps?" she asked.

"I have a cousin, also named Shmuel, who lives in Argentina," I replied. "He sends me stamps from there and from other South American countries. Also, I work at an importing company during the day, and we get letters from many nations. I'm the only one there with an interest in stamp collecting."

"How wonderful!" she enthused.

"Stamps excite me," I continued. "They're a window to the world! I am also intrigued by the business possibilities they represent."

"You know, Shmuel," my teacher said, "I occasionally return home to visit my family in India. I would be happy to bring you back some stamps from my next trip."

"I would welcome any new additions to my collection!" I exclaimed. She followed through on her offer, returning from a subsequent visit to India with stamps for me.

"Shmuel, you are such a surprising young man," she said. "What other fascinating facts are there to know about you?"

"I am also an avid chess fan," I replied.

Chess was very popular in Poland and Palestine. Most families owned a chess set, and there was no expense beyond that; a game required only two willing participants. I had often played with my uncles in Zhabinka and with all of my friends in Palestine.

"I hope one day to compete against one of the famed Russian players!" I added.

"I wish you luck in that dream," she said with a grin. "I hear the Russians are masters of the game." I never played a Russian but did participate in some school competitions.

I smiled and thanked her as I gathered my things. When I took a step out the door, she called to me.

"You know, I've heard you want to attend the university someday. Whenever you apply, let me know. I would be happy to write you a letter of recommendation."

I thanked her again and continued on my way. She was true to her word: when I later applied to universities, she wrote a very helpful letter on my behalf.

In my second year at school, a young leader from Hashomer Hatzair ("The Youth Guard") came to speak to all of the classes. Hashomer Hatzair was a socialist movement that focused on protecting young workers from being exploited. The representative invited us to attend a regular meeting of the group at a small house on Ben Gurion Street, named after David Ben-Gurion, who became the first prime minister of the State of Israel.

Almost a month later, on a Saturday, I went to the meeting to see for myself what Hashomer Hatzair had to offer. The crowd was a mix of young men and women. After everyone was seated, the leader gave a short lecture about the movement and its activities. He told us about the kibbutzim (plural of kibbutz) that the group had founded. The kibbutzim of Hashomer Hatzair were socialist communities based on the tenets of German philosophers Karl Marx and Friedrich Engels. All members were equal; each contributed according to his or her ability and received according to his or her needs.

At the end of the speech, the leader played the harmonica, and we all danced the hora (a traditional Israeli circle dance) and the krakowiak (a Polish dance similar to the polka). I enjoyed the whole day. The gathering was social, the music beautiful, the dancing fun, and the talk inspiring. I joined the group and began attending its weekly meetings. In the summer, we would gather on the beach to eat, dance, and sing around a campfire. I remained a member of Hashomer Hatzair until I graduated from high school.

Another group I joined was the Histadrut, a labor union established in 1920. I was entitled to join because I was employed. Membership gave me access to health care services under the Kupat Cholim, the union's health plan.

At this time, I began to spend my breaks with fellow members of Hashomer Hatzair at their kibbutzim, called Beit Alpha, Nir David, and Mishmar Haemek. I was put on the work schedule just like the other members. I labored in the fields, washed dishes in the kitchen, and cleaned the latrines. Dinner was served in the *hadar ochel* (dining hall) and consisted of bread, olive oil, green olives, vegetables, and vegetable soup. On Shabbat, we had chicken soup and fruit. Although Shabbat is a day of rest, Hashomer Hatzair was a secular organization, so there were no religious services. I enjoyed being part of the group and fulfilling my responsibilities.

Because most of the members of the kibbutzim were younger, we spent our nights outside singing and dancing, and playing music on the harmonica, accordion, and fiddle. At Nir David, after dancing, we would sometimes jump naked into a pond to take a swim. Occasionally, in the evenings, we listened to lectures about Marx, Engels, and Lenin. As I learned more about Communism, I realized that this ideology, which Hashomer Hatzair taught, ultimately

Marching (front left) in the Yom Hahistadrut (Israeli Labor Day) Parade, 1939

didn't work. (The movement of the former Soviet Union toward a capitalist society illustrates this point. China also now practices capitalism in certain aspects of its economy.)

My experiences with Hashomer Hatzair taught me that the doctrine of total equality cannot succeed, because every individual has different abilities, desires, and ambitions. When a kibbutz started with a group of young people, establishing equality among them was simple; being young and inexperienced, we had not yet identified our own strengths and wishes, so adults could easily tell us what to do. But as the kibbutz developed, those members with marketable skills received job opportunities *on behalf of* the kibbutz rather than *on* the kibbutz. These individuals, often talented in business, public speaking, and the arts, were excused from working in the fields, cleaning the latrines, and doing other manual labor. For example, the business manager, who was called the secretary, was permitted to eat meals outside of the kibbutz rather than with the other members in the dining hall. He or she was also rewarded with a car! This kind of special treatment undermined the sense of equality among kibbutz members.

A related development was the hiring of nonmembers to work on the kibbutz. Initially, the kibbutzim employed only their own members, making the communities self-sufficient. But as each kibbutz expanded in production and industry, it needed outside people to assist in its operations. These individuals were employed by the kibbutz but were not members of it—which added to the confusion surrounding equality.

As the kibbutzim grew, they transformed in other ways. One change related to the status of children. Once admitted, children were considered property of the kibbutz; as such, they were expected to live in communal children's houses. Parents who wanted to keep their children with them (as I think they rightly should be) resisted this mandate. Another significant change was in the approach to romantic partnerships. Initially, when two individuals were in a relationship, they were encouraged to live together but were not urged to marry, in keeping with the principle of "free love." When the two decided to part ways, they did so. A shift occurred, however, and couples who lived together began facing pressure to marry.

These and other issues had to be addressed in order for the kibbutzim of Hashomer Hatzair to be sustained. Still, despite the shortcomings of Communism, I recognized that the kibbutzim made important contributions. They helped the developing nation of Israel economically during its Palestine period, and also provided safety and protection to its members. These benefits can still be observed today.

I enjoyed my experience on the kibbutzim of Hashomer Hatzair and learned a lot from the time I spent there, but I did not lose sight of my goal to pursue a university education.

Chapter 8

Cigarettes and Coffee: Some Brotherly Advice

MY BROTHER, AT NINETEEN, was living on his own; he had moved out of our parents' home after graduating from high school. Avraham visited us from time to time, and was always respectful, but we rarely had the opportunity to discuss our respective beliefs. So I was pleased when he invited me to lunch one day on fashionable Dizengoff Street. I was seventeen at the time.

After we were seated at the restaurant, Avraham took out a pack of cigarettes and offered me one. I politely declined and added that I didn't smoke. He proceeded to take one out for himself, light it, and begin to offer some words of wisdom—though I'm not sure how much wisdom can be shared between two teenagers.

"You know, enjoying a cigarette is one of the pleasant things in life, and you're missing out on it!" he said. "You're always so busy, working all day and going to evening school. You don't have time to enjoy any of life's pleasures." He paused, took a puff, and continued. "These are your best years, and you are letting them pass you by!"

Avraham took a sip of his coffee and stared contemplatively at the people passing on the street before returning his attention to me.

"You've been working your whole life—in Warsaw as a child, in Petach Tikvah at the groves, in Kfar Hess on Uncle David's farm, and even on vacation at the kibbutzim! You never stop to enjoy life. You're missing a lot! But it isn't too late," he concluded.

I respected my brother's opinion but didn't attach much importance to it. I worked as a child because our family needed money. In Petach Tikvah, I labored to save money for myself, because I never wanted to experience hunger again. And my hard work on the farm brought me closer to my uncle and gave me the chance to see how a moshav worked. I learned valuable lessons from each of my jobs. I don't think my brother understood that.

Avraham shifted the discussion to his disapproval of Hashomer Hatzair. I knew my participation in the organization puzzled him. As I have mentioned, Hashomer Hatzair advocated Communism, a system that was contrary to our family's beliefs; so naturally, he disagreed with my involvement.

"Shmuel, I want you to know that the Soviet Union practices Communism, but actually, it's a dictatorship. All the talk about equality isn't being realized. Those who rule enjoy all the privileges of life, with beautiful villas, modern cars, and the finest foods, while the peasants work hard and barely have enough to sustain themselves. Furthermore, many who resist the Communist philosophy are being sent to Siberian labor camps—or worse."

"Avraham," I started, "I am familiar with most of what you have said, and I agree with you. I experienced what you just described on the kibbutzim, but Hashomer

Hatzair's practices are changing and adjusting to the real world. Although the kibbutzim have some flaws, they serve important functions here, namely offering protection, providing leaders and valuable support for the military, and improving the economy and other aspects of life."

He conceded with a nod and said, "Okay, but you should learn more about German authors and composers. Their works are amazingly beautiful. The poetry of Goethe and Schiller, and the music of Bach, Handel, and others—you should consider exploring them."

"That's a good idea," I replied, "because until now, I have paid more attention to Russian authors and composers, like Tolstoy and Tchaikovsky."

"Shmuel," he added, "I admire your dedication. Ever since you were very young, you have tried to help the family by working and making a contribution. But now it's time not only to enjoy yourself more but to plan for your future. As for me, I want to be a writer. I'm going to apply to work at the newspaper Haaretz. I think I have a very good chance for a career there."

I told him, "Right now, I know I want to continue my education past high school. Eventually, I want to attend the Hebrew University. My long-term goal is to become a teacher at the university and maybe also become an entrepreneur in international business."

He smiled. "Those are ambitious goals. Best of luck to you, brother! You will make a fine businessman someday."

With a hug and a handshake, we parted. From time to time afterward, we would meet briefly to catch up on each other's progress. Eventually, Avraham did become a writer and an editor at the major Israeli newspaper *Haaretz*. Regrettably, our conversation that day on Dizengoff Street was the most serious we ever had. We did enjoy a very lively exchange of correspondence, however, when I moved to California many years later.

Chapter 9

Food and Shelter: Aiding Jewish Refugees

HASHOMER HATZAIR WAS VERY SUPPORTIVE of Russia in World War II. Germany had already demonstrated its ruthlessness by signing a 1939 nonaggression pact with the Soviet Union, which divided Poland between them, and then invading the USSR less than two years later. Hitler intended to destroy the Communist state and the Soviet Jews. To me and to the Jewish refugees from Europe who were fortunate enough to make it to Palestine, it seemed as if the Nazis would do whatever it took to annihilate more Jews.

About nine months before Germany's invasion of the Soviet Union, on September 9, 1940, Tel Aviv was attacked by Italian bombers. The raid was part of a campaign by the Italian Royal Air Force against the United Kingdom. (At the time, Palestine was under British administration.) The aircraft dropped many bombs, and one fell very close to where I was at the time. I wasn't hurt, but 137 civilians died. Many buildings, both commercial and residential, were demolished. Much later, we learned that the Italians had been targeting the port of Haifa but were forced to change course when British fighter planes scrambled to meet them. The bombers were then ordered to strike British shipping facilities near Tel Aviv, but they missed, hitting civilian structures instead.

In February 1941, Field Marshal Erwin Rommel was appointed commander of the German military unit Afrika Korps. Rommel's daring tactics in North Africa earned him the nickname the "Desert Fox." In our Hashomer Hatzair meetings, we discussed that if Rommel was to advance into Egypt and take Alexandria, he would most likely continue toward Palestine. The leaders of our group proposed a plan to flee to Russia and even volunteer to join the Russian army, which began fighting the Nazis in June 1941. We were relieved when, in November 1942, British field marshal Bernard Montgomery defeated Rommel's forces in western Egypt, forcing the Afrika Korps to retreat.

In the latter part of the war, I simply could *not* carry on with life as usual. The escalating danger of war in Palestine was always on my mind. I felt compelled to join the Haganah ("The Defense" in Hebrew). The Haganah was a Jewish paramilitary organization in the British Mandate of Palestine—the geopolitical entity administered by the British from 1920 to 1948 that served, in part, as a national home for the Jewish people. The Haganah later became the core of the Israel Defense Forces, which has guarded the State of Israel since 1948.

The Haganah was preparing specifically to meet threats from Jewish Palestine's Arab neighbors, led by the Grand Mufti of Jerusalem, Muhammad Amin al-Husayni—an active opponent of Zionism. At the beginning of each week, the officer of my unit would give me a schedule telling me when to report for training on the weekend. I was learning the topography of the country; we needed to know where we could be attacked and how to defend each area. I also learned how to shoot different types of guns.

As the Nazi regime was spreading across Poland and other countries, with its message of anti-Semitism, Jewish families in Palestine, including my own, grew increasingly concerned about the safety of our loved ones in Europe. In the later years of the war, we became aware of the horrors of the Holocaust. Painfully, we saw countries that could easily have provided safety for Jewish refugees turn them away.

In 1917, the Balfour Declaration had stated that the British government viewed "with favour the establishment in Palestine of a national home for the Jewish people [with the understanding that] nothing shall be done which may prejudice the civil and religious rights of the existing non-Jewish communities in Palestine." A 1939 policy paper by the British (the British White Paper of 1939), however, severely limited Jewish immigration to Palestine for the years 1940 to 1944. Whether or not the refugees were admitted into Palestine would likely determine if they lived or died. It would also impact the survival of the Jewish community. If granted entrance, these immigrants would build up the Jewish population in Palestine and make it stronger. Therefore, legal technicalities simply could not be allowed to keep Europe's Jews out. We knew it was up to us, the pre-war settlers of Palestine, to rescue them.

The Haganah used all the means we could, including ruses, to get around Britain's policy. One criterion for granting Jewish immigrants permission to enter was if their spouses were already living in Palestine. So some of the Jews in Palestine forged marriage certificates, traveled to Europe, and brought their "spouses" back with them. For those who returned, this effort was extremely gratifying—but horrifying. They were able to save some of their family members but simply could not save them all. Many friends and fellow settlers recounted to me the specifics about which relatives they were able to bring with them, and which ones they were forced, heartbroken, to leave behind. Unfortunately, most of those who remained in Europe perished.

Like Britain in regard to Palestine, the United States had very strict quotas on Jewish immigration. The U.S. government feared that some individuals coming from Europe could be working as agents for Germany, so it placed stringent restrictions on entry. The American public also opposed Jewish immigration, due to economic depression, fear of foreigners, and anti-Semitism. By January 1944, however, the evidence of the mass murder of European Jews was irrefutable, and President Franklin D. Roosevelt finally took action to save them.

When World War II ended in Europe and the Middle East in May 1945, the Haganah made every effort to bring surviving Jews into Palestine. Still faced with the immigration restrictions imposed by the British White Paper of 1939, which had been extended, we again had to devise ways of getting around them. From 1941 to 1948, more than any other group, the Haganah orchestrated the safe transport of Jews into Palestine. But for the Haganah, the refugees would have been on their own, struggling to survive; many would have perished. Indeed, some ships carrying refugees were caught by the British navy and turned away from Palestine.

They were sent to Cyprus, where the refugees were stuck in crowded detention camps indefinitely. I was personally so incensed that the British government would not open the ports of Haifa and Jaffa to the Jewish refugees that I dedicated myself to getting these displaced persons into Palestine.

Every day, ships filled with Jews from Europe approached the shores of Palestine. They were directed toward obscure harbors unguarded by the British. In the late-night hours, under the cover of night, the boats dropped anchor a distance from shore. The members of the Haganah could not make use of rowboats or rubber life rafts, which might have drawn attention to the operation. Instead, we waded or swam out to the boat and helped the refugees into the water. Most of them were very weak from the concentration camps and terrified of the cold, dark sea. We didn't have life preservers to give them, so with great exertion and with strength we didn't know we had, we pulled the refugees—men, women, and children—to shore. These nighttime rescue scenes remain permanently etched in my memory.

As I mentioned, when I was a young boy in Zhabinka, my cousins took me swimming in the Mukhavets River. I always enjoyed this pastime. Our apartment in Tel Aviv was just a short walk from the shore of the Mediterranean, and I spent any free time I had swimming. I was a strong and confident swimmer in open water, but I knew the risks—firsthand. One morning, very early, I was swimming by myself off the coast near Tel Aviv. Suddenly, I realized I was caught in a powerful undertow, being swept farther and farther out to sea. I called for help, but there was no one else in the water or on the beach. Really scared, I kept screaming for assistance. Thankfully, at about 6:00 a.m., a lifeguard arriving at his post heard me. He swam out, and together, we struggled back to shore. Had he not appeared when he did, I would have been in grave danger. Eventually, I also trained to be a lifeguard, which provided me with additional summer employment opportunities.

With my near drowning always in the back of my mind, I carried the feeble, fearful, despairing passengers to land. Of course, at night, along the deserted beaches between Haifa and Tel Aviv, there were no lifeguards keeping watch. By the time we reached shore, the refugees were shivering and exhausted. In my experience, however, no one ever drowned—a true miracle.

After a brief rest, we would gather the refugees and hike to the nearest kibbutz, where food and shelter were provided. We continued these daring missions for some time. While I was with the Haganah, we safely brought in over 20,000 Jewish refugees, from both big cities and small villages. They came from just about every country in Europe, speaking many different languages. Most did not know Hebrew, but many spoke Yiddish, allowing us to communicate with each other.

Both kibbutzim and moshavim welcomed the new arrivals. Although the two types of settlements had significant differences, both were completely unlike the shtetls and cities from which the immigrants had come. In Europe, very few Jews had been farmers. In Palestine, however, they had little choice but to work the land. Former townspeople—shopkeepers, craftsmen, tradesmen, religious students—suddenly learned how to be farmers, out of necessity. Later, unfortunately, they would learn how to be soldiers, also out of necessity.

Increasing tension between the Arabs and the Jews in Palestine sparked violent conflicts, so defending the kibbutzim, moshavim, and surrounding communities from harm grew more important. As part of the Haganah, I was responsible for providing this protection. During the evening hours, I would report to my assigned kibbutz, where I sometimes partnered with one of the residents or another member of the Haganah. Armed with guns, we would patrol the kibbutz and the surrounding area together. It occurred to me that I had never carried a gun before. Neither had my father, or anyone else in my family.

Although my patrols never involved gun battles, they were nevertheless quite tense. For example, it was not easy to tell right away if two figures walking in the dark were teenagers seeking romantic time alone or armed men scouting the terrain to plan an attack. We devised methods to quickly identify the people we encountered. For instance, we implemented passwords, which only members of the kibbutz knew. We would shout out the key words, and wait for the appropriate response from the unknown individuals.

On these nighttime rounds, I had plenty of time to think about the amazing transition of the Jewish refugees from passive, insular, obedient, sometimes helpless souls to modern Israeli citizen-soldiers, carrying guns and bravely facing danger. From my teenage years to my mid-twenties, I also matured tremendously. Several avenues were now available to me to work and earn money. Though I was by no means financially well-off, I felt confident in my ability to find employment and support myself. I realized I would encounter many obstacles on the road to my goals, but after witnessing the transformation of the refugees, I knew sheer determination would be an essential component of my success.

I also came to recognize that in addition to taking care of myself and my family, I had a civic responsibility to my country. A democratic state provides the freedoms, rights, and protections that enable its people to pursue their dreams. In turn, I learned to appreciate my role as a citizen.

We in the Haganah helped facilitate the exodus of Jewish refugees from Eastern Europe to British Palestine, soon to become the State of Israel. Leon Uris's 1958 book Exodus provides a stunning narrative of this time in Palestine's history. The story was brought to an even wider audience with the 1960 screen adaptation, starring Paul Newman in the role of a Haganah member. Both the book and the film were quite influential in the United States, stimulating support for Israel. The movie, in particular, is often credited with having a tremendous impact on American views of Israel and issues in the Middle East.

I believe it is essential for Jews to have a country of their own after the suffering they have endured since the Diaspora—the scattering of the Jewish people outside their homeland following exile in 597 BCE. I was honored to serve in the Haganah and make my own modest contribution to the rescue of Jews and the establishment of the State of Israel.

Chapter 10

Cocoa Beans from Ceylon: Taking Initiative

ABOUT TWO YEARS AFTER THE OUTBREAK of World War II, I graduated from the Gymnasium Erev. I was nineteen. Throughout high school, I had worked full-time for Green Brothers. After two years as a delivery boy, I was promoted to a job in the office of the president's secretary. Because the company relied heavily on imports from Europe, many divisions suffered as a result of the war. Therefore, Green Brothers had to expand the types of merchandise it was importing. I went to the public library on Hayarkon Street and used the *Encyclopaedia Britannica* to research countries that were producing goods that could be of use to the people in Palestine. I looked for goods from regions unaffected by the conflict.

I knew there was a big demand for chocolate. I contacted a firm in Ceylon (now Sri Lanka) that harvested and sold cocoa beans, used in the manufacturing of chocolate. The president of Green Brothers was surprised and pleased by my initiative. I acquired samples of almost a dozen varieties of cocoa beans. They arrived by parcel post, packaged in mesh bags roughly the size of an orange.

I took the samples to Elite, the biggest candy manufacturer in the region. The buyer had never encountered such a variety of cocoa beans. I made him a competitive offer, and he placed a sizable order with me. As a bonus of sorts, the representatives from Elite presented me with a pair of large chocolate bricks made from the samples I had offered them.

As the war went on, Green Brothers continued to suffer. Many employees were let go. I kept working in my department, however, which had now expanded to include the export of my favorite product—Jaffa oranges.

I sought additional sources for goods that would be in high demand in Palestine. A friend of mine who had recently traveled to France told me about Rodier Fabrics, a Paris company that manufactured fine textiles. I sent them a letter of introduction, asking if they would be interested in exporting their merchandise to Palestine. I received a very favorable response from the director, Mr. Le Conte, who provided information about the types of fabrics they produced. I replied that I would be pleased to be an agent for Rodier through Green Brothers in Palestine. I also requested samples and a price list, which I received through the post office. I showed the samples to some of the fabric stores in Tel Aviv and, to my delight, got several orders within the first few weeks.

A few months later, Mr. Le Conte and his wife traveled to Palestine. During his visit, Mr. Le Conte called on several of my customers with me. The director of Green Brothers, Mr. Cohen, arranged for me and Mr. and Mrs. Le Conte to join him and his wife for dinner and dancing on a boat on the Yarkon River. The evening was delightful. The business between Rodier Fabrics and Green Brothers flourished. When I left Israel to go to college in America, I wrote to Mr. Le Conte about my plans. I told him I intended to be in touch with him after I completed my studies.

Despite my success at Green Brothers, I remained determined to pursue higher education. The waiting lists at the two universities in Israel were extremely long, so I sought other options until I could gain entrance. I enrolled at the British Institute. It wasn't a full university but offered classes in the evenings that would help me with my business pursuits. The British government established such institutes in the countries they occupied in order to have a greater influence on the local population. The class offerings consisted of material relating exclusively to English culture, in particular language, speech, literature, and history. I initially took English language and speech classes. The teachers, all of whom were British, treated us respectfully—unlike the soldiers and police who controlled Palestine.

On the first day of speech class, after introducing himself, the teacher asked us about our origins and native languages. The young lady sitting next to me raised her hand and said, "I'm from Lvov, and I speak Polish." I then raised my hand and said, "I'm from Warsaw, and I also speak Polish." She looked at me, and I noticed that she was very attractive. When the class was over, she approached me.

"My name is Olga. What's yours?"

"I'm Shmuel," I replied.

"Well, Shmuel, since you are from Poland, you must be familiar with our composer Chopin," she said.

"I am familiar with his work, and I am fond of it," I said.

"One of my friends will be performing his music at her home on Rothschild Boulevard tonight. Would you like to join me?" she asked.

"I'd be very happy to," I answered.

We met up later and set out for her friend's home, which was nearby. Speaking in Polish, we got to know each other as we walked. She told me about her family, and I told her about mine. When we arrived at our destination, there were about a dozen people conversing in Polish. We took our seats to listen to the performance, which was very enjoyable. Afterward, Olga asked me to accompany her home, which I gladly did. When we parted, she invited me to join her that Saturday night at Pinati, a coffeehouse on Dizengoff Street that was a popular hangout for young people. I accepted. Luckily for us, the coffeehouse played classical music from a phonograph on Saturday evenings. That date was the start of a warm and loving relationship that lasted seven or eight years.

I was three years older than Olga, who, at the time that we met, was about sixteen. In addition to being beautiful, she was smart and thoughtful. We talked about our ambitions, and we shared our ideas about life. She strongly supported my goals and encouraged me to pursue them with great haste. When I asked if she would also attend the university, she shook her head.

"I wish I could join you there," she began, "but I don't think my parents would let me. I'm their only child, and they expect me to help with the family business."

Around this time, I finally took my brother's advice to enjoy life. So in addition to working hard, I engaged in some pleasurable activities. Olga and I regularly attended concerts conducted by the Palestine Symphony Orchestra and frequently returned to Pinati to listen to classical music on the phonograph. In the spring and summer, I would sometimes take time off from work to walk along the Yarkon River or to exercise on the beach. For the first time in my life, I didn't focus completely on work. This approach was new, but I liked it.

Several weeks after we met, Olga introduced me to her group of friends, all of whom were from Poland. Their families, just like mine, had immigrated to Palestine to escape anti-Semitism and to find better economic opportunities. Although all of these young people were Jewish, they were not especially religious or spiritual; they didn't follow the traditional practices the way I did with my family. None of them worked, although some were students.

Olga and I along the Yarkon River, Tel Aviv, February 1949

I was cordial to all of Olga's friends, because they were very nice, but my friendliness was sometimes misconstrued: some of the girls let me know that they desired a closer relationship with me. I was surprised by their forwardness. Perhaps they thought I would make a good husband because of my looks, pleasant attitude, or serious job. Whatever the appeal, I had no interest in pursuing anything more than friendship with them. I remained loyal to Olga, whom I came to appreciate more and more as time went by.

I was so busy working, going to school, and visiting with Olga that I didn't realize I was being observed. My mother had noticed the changes in my behavior and attitude. One evening when I came home, she took me aside.

"I hear you have developed a close relationship with a Polish girl," she said. "Your uncle Pesach told me he saw you a couple of times walking hand in hand."

Not one to lie, I explained the situation. "Yes, *Ema*, I have met a young lady. Her name is Olga. She is Jewish and attends the British Institute with me."

My mother drew in a breath but remained without any clear expression. She did not appear angry, surprised, hurt, or displeased. Maybe she was processing what I had just told her. Before excusing me, she patted me on the shoulder and said, "That's okay, Shmuel." As I departed for my room, she added, "I may have a surprise for you sometime this week, so don't forget to spend some time here at home."

I wasn't certain what my mother was aiming to do, but she had a habit of being a matchmaker. She had gotten several of my cousins together, with the goal of maintaining the closeness of the family.

On Shabbat afternoon, my mother asked me to stay after lunch. Soon, I heard a knock. Opening the front door, I was surprised to find my cousin Shulamit, the daughter of my uncle David in Kfar Hess. I greeted her with a warm shalom and invited her in. Shulamit looked and acted just like a farmer's daughter. She was tall, about my height, and strong, with muscles all over her body. She had changed dramatically since I last visited my uncle some years earlier. She had grown into an attractive young woman, but she was not my type. I remained courteous, however, because I was aware of my mother's intentions, and Shulamit was family.

"Do you still live with your dad?" I asked.

"I do. I love farm life," she answered. "I plan to live on a kibbutz or a moshav. One day, I hope to have my own farm."

"As you know, I worked on your father's farm several times," I replied. "I know farming can be a pleasant life. As for me, I have other goals."

I didn't get too close to Shulamit, to avoid sending the message that I was interested. I invited her out for a walk, and we stopped on Allenby Street for tea and cake. She stayed with us overnight. The next day, I walked her to the bus station so she could go back to Kfar Hess. I returned home, and my mother greeted me as I entered the apartment.

"Shmuel," she said excitedly, "I hope you had a nice time with Shulamit! Isn't she a lovely and pleasant young lady? The daughter of your favorite uncle—wouldn't it be nice if you were to meet her again and get to know her better?"

Even though I completely disagreed with my mother's plan to match me with my cousin, out of respect, I said, "I will give it some thought. Thank you for inviting her."

After that, I saw Shulamit whenever we visited my uncle. But our relationship never developed past friendship.

Chapter 11

Cut Off from Food and Water: Saving Jerusalem

ON NOVEMBER 29, 1947, the United Nations General Assembly adopted a resolution terminating the British Mandate of Palestine and recommending the adoption and implementation of a plan to divide Palestine into independent Arab and Jewish states. This plan, called the Plan of Partition with Economic Union, also called for Jerusalem to be placed under international rule, due to the city's global importance.

The partition plan was accepted by the Jewish public and by the Jewish Agency for Palestine (later the Jewish Agency for Israel), an organization that would play a dominant role in establishing and building the State of Israel. The plan was rejected, however, by Arab leaders and governments; they would not agree to any type of territorial division.

On May 14, 1948, David Ben-Gurion, executive head of the World Zionist Organization and head of the Jewish Agency for Palestine, proclaimed "the establishment of a Jewish state in *Eretz Yisrael*, to be known as the State of Israel." Ben-Gurion had selected the name "Israel" for the new state, and all members of the provisional government accepted it. On the same day, Ben-Gurion was the first to sign the Israeli Declaration of Independence, which he had helped write.

I remember the day of Ben-Gurion's proclamation very clearly. I was still working at Green Brothers, as manager of the import department. That Friday morning, I met my three best friends from high school—David, Reuben, and Yosef—at a coffeehouse in Tel Aviv. We had a very serious conversation about what we were going to do after Ben-Gurion's announcement, which was expected shortly. We agreed that we would volunteer for the army.

Along with hundreds of other Jews, we went to stand in front of an art museum on Rothschild Boulevard, where Ben-Gurion was going to announce the birth of the State of Israel. Fittingly, the museum came to be known as Independence Hall. As we waited, "Hatikvah" ("The Hope")—the anthem of the Jewish people—began playing through loudspeakers. Soon, everyone on the boulevard was singing. A tremendous feeling of positive energy enveloped the crowd. After being exiled from our ancient homeland more than two thousand years earlier, we were about to witness the rebirth of the Jewish state.

Suddenly, the music stopped, and the broadcast of Ben-Gurion came on. In an eloquent and passionate speech, he described the long journey the Jewish people had faced; the suffering we had endured; and our unwavering faith, which fueled our continued efforts to establish a place where all Jews would be welcome. His words expressed everything that was in our hearts, and when he announced that the State of Israel was born, the crowd burst into a jubilant roar.

How overjoyed we were to have our own homeland! The Palestine Symphony Orchestra played "Hatikvah" again, and the entire mass of people started dancing the hora—as I had done many times on the kibbutz and with my family many years earlier. We danced in the streets until midnight!

The day after Ben-Gurion's announcement, on May 15, 1948, the Arab–Israeli War began. Five neighboring Arab states invaded the former Palestinian mandate and attacked Jewish settlements.

Filled with patriotism, I returned home to my parents that Saturday and announced, "I am not going to wait for the Haganah to ask me to join the Israeli army. I am going to do it myself tomorrow!"

My parents expressed some concern but respected my decision. "I pray that God may protect you," my father said.

On Sunday, along with some sixty other young men, I waited in line at one of the many recruiting centers in Tel Aviv to enlist in the Israel Defense Forces. Unlike today's rigorous standards for health and intelligence, the requirements for service in the IDF were quite lax; unless you had a grave malady, you were almost certain to be accepted.

I had arrived a little later than my three friends, who were already in line. A messenger then appeared from the Israeli Air Force, requesting fourteen people to fill immediate vacancies. Recruits were pulled from the back of the line—and that was how I became separated from my friends and part of the air force.

I think back on that morning with both pride and sadness. Of my three friends, only David survived the War of Independence. Reuben and Yosef perished. Our fates seemed to have been determined that day. I still feel that if I had been at the front of the line, and inducted into the ground troops instead of the air force, I would have died. I will always miss my two friends, and others, who gave their lives so that the State of Israel could endure. Recalling their sacrifice is incredibly painful.

After passing the air force's physical examination, I was sent to Tzrifin, which had been a British base called Sarafand during World War I. There, I was assigned to the supply depot. Our warehouses did not have a big inventory, but trucks soon began arriving with aircraft equipment left over from the British forces that had enforced the mandate. We also had several light planes that were manufactured in England. They were nicknamed "Primus" because they made a loud noise similar to that of a popular pressurized-burner kerosene stove of the same name. Soon, however, much larger aircraft arrived from Czechoslovakia with the necessary equipment and spare parts.

Eventually, experienced aviators from Great Britain, Canada, and the United States came to help train our young pilots. These individuals were typically retired air force or commercial pilots who were committed to helping the fledgling Jewish state survive. Another group of training pilots consisted of Israelis who had been trained by the United Kingdom's Royal Air Force (RAF) to help fight Nazi Germany. Among these British-trained pilots was Ezer Weizman, who would go on to become commander of the Israeli Air Force and the seventh president of Israel. He had been trained in Great Britain and Rhodesia, and served with the Royal Air Force in India.

One military effort that stands out in my memory is the Battle for Jerusalem. It had begun in December 1947, immediately following the adoption of the partition plan. The Jewish and Arab people, and later the Israeli and Jordanian armies, fought to control the city. In February 1948, the Jordanian army blockaded the road that allowed supplies to reach Jerusalem's Jewish population. Our people were cut off from food and water, and the situation became desperate.

Ben-Gurion felt that saving Jerusalem was the military's most important responsibility. But Yigael Yadin, head of the Israel Defense Forces, didn't want to lose troops to the Jordanian army when Egyptian forces were advancing from the south. Ben-Gurion prevailed. Between May and July 1948, the Israel Defense Forces and the Jordanian Arab Legion engaged in an incredibly difficult string of military engagements, the Battles of Latrun—in which Israel was ultimately unable to capture the strategic hilltop above the road from Tel Aviv to Jerusalem. Regrettably, my very dear friends were lost during the siege of Jerusalem, which ended in June 1948 with the opening of a makeshift road that allowed supplies to get through to the city.

I worked very hard in the air force, often ten to twelve hours a day, every day, because there were a limited number of people on our base. At first, I was in charge of communicating with the headquarters of the air force in Tel Aviv. Then I was promoted to staff sergeant and put in charge of inventory control. The second year, I became assistant to the colonel of the facility. Among my duties was acting as a judge on a panel that decided punishments for misdeeds. I took this important responsibility very seriously.

In my military uniform on the beach in Tel Aviv, 1949

The colonel urged me to stay in the air force and be promoted to captain, working directly with him. I seriously considered this option, but I knew I could not be a career soldier. I was determined to go to college, and thus to create new opportunities for myself. Now was the time to follow my dreams. Though grateful to my commanding officer, I respectfully declined his offer. I explained my goals, and he wished me much success. I chose a life of peace over war, and I'm very glad I did. I stayed on as a member of the air force until the war was over and we were decommissioned.

Several truces were attempted during the course of the conflict but didn't hold. The war lasted for almost ten months, until March 10, 1949, with Israel defeating the Palestinian Arabs and a coalition of Arab states. After Israel signed armistices with Egypt, Lebanon, Jordan, and Syria, the state's territory included about 75 percent of the prior British mandate.

Arab casualties in the war numbered roughly seven thousand. Israel lost over six thousand people, or about 1 percent of its population. Approximately two thousand had been Holocaust survivors. I felt that others who served in the military during the war faced many more dangers than I did.

David Ben-Gurion led Israel during the War of Independence, and united various groups and organizations into the Israel Defense Forces. In 1948, he became the first prime minister and first defense minister of Israel. Consequently, he has become known as Israel's founding father.

Chapter 12

The Coffee House: Chance Encounters

NOT LONG AFTER I ENLISTED in the air force, Olga did the same. Perhaps she was trying to stay close to me, but with our busy schedules, we rarely saw each other. She worked at the Israeli Air Force headquarters on Hayarkon Street, in Tel Aviv, where Ezer Weizman and the other chiefs were stationed.

When I returned home to civilian life, I began to think about how to reach my goals of getting a university education and becoming an international entrepreneur. Olga was planning to return to Poland, and I had to consider her place in my life. We met at Pinati to talk. Sitting across from her, I noticed that she seemed somewhat different than when we first met. She wasn't as vibrant or energetic as before but seemed more aggressive and less compromising.

We spoke about our experiences during the war, and our future plans. My thoughts were of continuing my education. Olga's thoughts went a different way.

"I want to get married," she announced.

I processed her declaration, pondering how best to say that I wasn't going to marry her. There's no easy way to tell someone you've spent years with that you don't share the same intention for the relationship.

"I'm sorry, Olga," I said, "but I don't want to get married. At least not anytime soon."

"But why not? Have I done something wrong?" she asked.

"No, nothing of the sort," I said. "Our lives are taking separate paths now. I may study abroad. You are going back to Poland with your parents."

"But you could study in Warsaw! You could pursue your education there! Why won't you come with me?" she asked.

"I don't know where I'll end up," I began. "I may go to Europe. I may go to the United States. I can't make you a promise when I don't know where I might go to create a future for myself."

Sadness weighed down her face. I felt heaviness in my heart, too.

"So this is it?" she asked, her eyes filling with tears. "This is how it ends?"

I couldn't bear to see her so unhappy. I looked down, struggling to keep my own sorrow from overtaking me. Despite the difficulty of the circumstances, I had to stay strong. I didn't want to hurt her, but I knew I couldn't avoid it.

"I'm sorry," I said, "but this is the way it must end."

A long silence followed. Olga looked at me imploringly, as if pleading for me to reconsider my decision. But I knew I had to follow my dreams. I couldn't make a life for myself doing what someone else wanted.

A pair of heavy sighs broke the silence, followed by the low screech of chairs moving backward. We stood and stepped closer to each other. She gave me a warm and strong embrace, and kissed me. Then we left, going in different directions. I never saw her again.

At this time, I redoubled my efforts to get a higher education. The first of several obstacles was the closure of the Hebrew University, on Mount Scopus in Jerusalem. As part of the 1949 armistice with Jordan, Jordanian forces controlled the land where the school was—and the campus was closed to students and visitors. Caretakers were allowed to enter occasionally, to keep the facilities clean and operable.

The only other university in Israel was the Technion, located in Haifa. It had opened in 1924 as an institute of engineering and sciences. The enormously long waiting list at the school was a second obstacle. The unlikeliness of being admitted didn't especially disappoint me, however, because the Technion lacked the economics and international business courses I was looking to take.

I also explored my options outside of Israel, sending applications to universities in England, France, Switzerland, and the United States. To my surprise, all of them were willing to accept me—but each required up to $250 in fees and tuition per semester. I didn't have the money.

During my time in the service, I spent much of what I had saved while working at Green Brothers. The salaries of soldiers were very low, so I hardly had enough to sustain myself. Following the Arab–Israeli War, the economy of Israel continued to be difficult. Many families struggled to buy what they needed to live, and I knew I couldn't count on help from my own family.

I decided to ponder solutions to my money problem over a cup of tea at Pinati. I arrived just before a rush of customers and was fortunate to find a table. Just as I was starting to contemplate my situation, a man interrupted me.

"Excuse me," he said in English. "May I join you?"

I nodded and gestured for him to take a seat.

He thanked me and sat down. Then he extended his hand. "How do you do, sir? My name's Bob. Nice to meet you."

"I'm Shami," I said, shaking his hand. "What brings you to Israel?"

"I'm an airline pilot from America," he explained. "I'm out here frequently for business."

"A pilot!" I said. "That must be exciting. I recently served in the Israeli Air Force, although I never became a pilot."

"Well, isn't that something!" he proclaimed.

We continued to converse about the military, my service, flying, and the United States. Despite my courses at the British Institute, my English was broken. Bob didn't speak any other languages, though, so we communicated the best we could. I asked if he wanted another cup of tea, and he did. I called out to the waiter.

Hearing me place the order, Bob asked, "You speak Hebrew?"

"Yes, I do," I responded.

He thought for a moment and then said, "Maybe you can help me."

"How could I help you?" I asked, curious.

"I often pass through Tel Aviv on the way to Saudi Arabia. When I'm there, I buy gold coins. When I come back here, I exchange some of them on the black market—it offers a much better exchange rate than a bank."

I knew about the black-market zone on Lilienblum Street.

He went on. "I need someone who speaks Hebrew, so I know I'm not getting swindled. I'd give you 10 percent of what I make."

Without hesitation, I agreed to assist him. We shook hands and continued enjoying our tea.

Over the next few weeks, I helped Bob complete several transactions and earned almost $200. It wasn't quite enough to get into any of the universities that had accepted me, but it was a good start.

About a month after I met Bob, luck struck again at Pinati. I was meeting some friends there, and one brought along a young Jewish woman named Lillian. She and her family had fled from Poland to Russia, to escape Nazi persecution. Eventually, they made their way to China, which had accepted many refugees when Palestine and the United States imposed restrictions.

When she heard about my goal to attend university, she exclaimed, "I have great news for you! Have you heard about California? The Golden State? There's a college there, in a small city, called Tuft. It charges very little. My boyfriend, John, is an American soldier. He told me about this lovely place and how he wants to take me there. It's the paradise of California!"

I considered Lillian's words. That evening, I wrote a letter of application to Tuft College. To my great surprise, two weeks later, I received an uplifting letter from the director. He not only invited me to attend the college but offered me free tuition and free textbooks, and a six-dollar monthly fee for the dormitory (which could be waived if I worked on campus).

When I presented the letter to my parents and my uncle, they were also very surprised. One of my uncles undermined my excitement by saying that the offer was so good it probably wasn't real. He added, "Not many Americans actually keep their word, so be very cautious before accepting this invitation."

To determine whether the offer was genuine, I wrote another letter to the college. I requested more information about the school and its departments, especially the programs in which I was most interested. I also visited the American consulate in Tel Aviv. I told the official who greeted me, "I'd like to find out about Tuft College in California, and the city where it is located."

"I've never heard of that college," he replied. "However, we have a catalog of all the universities in the United States. I'll go take a look."

He came back a few minutes later. "Mr. Rimmon," he said, "I have good news for you. I couldn't find a *Tuft* College in California, but I was able to find a *Taft* College. It's a community college, which means you would study there for two years before transferring to a traditional four-year university."

I thanked him for the information. Then we chatted about our lives and experiences; I shared my educational goals. Toward the end of the conversation, he said, "You sound like a very focused individual. If you decide to go to California, or any other place to study, I'll provide you with a visa."

With that, we shook hands, and I departed. As I walked away, I heard him yell out, "I hope to see you soon!"

Having no options to continue my education in Israel, and recalling the enthusiasm with which Lillian had spoken of California, I made up my mind to go to Taft. If I did well there, I would hopefully be able to transfer to one of several state universities in Los Angeles. I shared my decision with my parents and a few other family members. My father offered me his insights.

"Shmuel," he said, "this could be a risky endeavor. But I know you want to be a university student. You have always worked hard—as a child in Warsaw, and as a young man at Green Brothers. I believe you will achieve your objective, but it won't be easy."

Not everyone was as supportive as my father. A cousin of my mother's was much more doubtful about my prospects. He tried to discourage me from going to America. He told me, "I've heard and read a bit about the United States. People go there with big dreams, and they work very hard. Even with continuous effort, it takes them a long time to achieve their dreams. Many are unsuccessful. Why don't you wait? Continue your work here, until the Jordanian military leaves. Then the Hebrew University will reopen. It may take a few years, but at least you'll be home."

I told him that I didn't want to wait any longer, was willing to take the risk, and would face whatever obstacles I encountered.

On New Year's Eve, 1949, my friends and I gathered to say farewell. We met at one of the very few hotels that existed in Tel Aviv at the time. It was on Hayarkon Street, overlooking the Mediterranean. We enjoyed dinner and then danced to a live orchestra late into the night.

The next day, my relatives came to my parents' apartment on Shenkin Street. We had a nice conversation about my future in the United States, and they wished me well.

Chapter 13

Third-Class Dining: Sailing to the United States

THE MORNING OF JANUARY 3, 1950, I got on a bus to Haifa, accompanied by my parents, brother, and sister. I had just turned twenty-seven. I was to board the SS *LaGuardia*, a former military ship that had been converted to a commercial passenger liner. The vessel was bound for New York City. At the port, each member of my family gave me a big hug and a kiss. As I walked up the ramp, I felt apprehensive and alone. A metal suitcase was all I had to start my new life with. It contained just a few shirts, a couple pairs of shorts, a jacket and pants, and my military uniform—humble provisions for such a grand adventure! As I made my way on deck, I was encouraged to see other young people who were probably also students; perhaps I would have company on my journey after all.

I found my room, which I was to share with five other people. The small cabin in steerage was simply furnished, with a triple bunk at each end, a table in the middle, and a small jug of water for all of us to share. The bathroom was too tiny to serve the needs of six occupants, but there wasn't anything we could do about it.

As we trickled in, we introduced ourselves and stated where we were heading. All of us were students, going to different places—some to New York City, others to Berkeley. After the introductions, we went up on deck, where we ran into other students. We all gathered near the railing and waved to our families on the docks. Soon, the ship pulled away from port, moving into the deep blue Mediterranean Sea.

Those in steerage were not allowed to go onto the ship's other levels, only on deck. There was little space to move around in the cabin, and several of us were sick from the rocking of the ship in the stormy winter waters. So we spent our time outside, on the deck, except during meals.

Our first stop was Athens, Greece, where the ship took on additional passengers. We remained in port for two days. I was thrilled to be on land again and visited many historical sites. While in Athens, I became acquainted with another student, Israel Szafir. He was planning to attend the University of California at Berkeley. I told him about the exceptional opportunity awaiting me at Taft College. He was surprised by the magnitude of the offer I received.

Sightseeing in Athens, 1950. (I am seated behind the woman wearing a headscarf.)

"It sounds almost too good to be true," he remarked. He asked to see the director's letter. After reading it, he said, "Based on what you have told me about this place—this paradise in California—I think I may join you there. As a foreign student, I'll have to pay $200 a semester at Berkeley, but it would be better if I didn't have to pay anything!"

"I would be very pleased if you joined me," I said. "I am confident you would be able to get in, if you have already been accepted at Berkeley."

We agreed to go to Taft together and enjoyed the rest of the day exploring the towns near Athens.

Several evenings later, a pair of women sat down next to me at dinner. Given their respective ages, I figured they were mother and daughter.

"Hello," the younger woman said. "My name is Effie. This is my mother." With a nudge, she whispered, "You'll have to excuse her. She doesn't speak English."

"My name is Shmuel," I said, "but everyone calls me Shami. I'm from Israel. I'm on my way to study in California. What about you?"

"We are from Greece," she said, "from the town of Thessaloniki. We are going to Canada. I have been admitted to study at McGill University, in Montreal. Where will you be studying?"

"At Taft College," I replied.

"Shami, I have never heard of this college," she said. "Are you sure it isn't Tufts University?"

"Many people have thought that," I said, "but Tufts isn't in California. Taft College is located in the city of Taft, in California." I went on to explain how I had heard about the school, the letter from the director, and my visit to the consulate. She was intrigued and asked to see the letter.

Effie on deck during the Atlantic crossing

The next day, Effie came up on deck to where I usually spent time. She shared with me her dream of going to a university, which was very similar to mine—although she was more interested in history and political science. After reading the letter, she tried to convince me to attend McGill with her. She recommended that I transfer there after going to Taft for a semester or two. She gushed about how wonderful the university was and added that it had an excellent program in international economics.

Our next port of call was Naples, Italy. Effie and her mother invited me to join them on a tour of the ruins of Pompeii and Herculaneum, ancient towns that had been buried in the eruption of Mount Vesuvius in 79 CE. Afterward, we shopped for souvenirs and mementos. They helped me choose some rosaries to give as gifts in the United States. I bartered for the rosaries with American cigarettes, which I had bought on the ship. Due to their extremely limited supply in Italy, cigarettes proved a valuable commodity.

After we left Italy, the voyage got more tumultuous. It rained constantly, and the waters of the Atlantic were horribly choppy. Passengers on deck were advised to remain near the rear of the ship, but most of us spent our time hanging over the rail, losing our battle with seasickness. To my surprise, Effie comforted me during my bouts of mal de mer. We became friends and spent quite a few hours together. She was very pleasant company, and her companionship made the trip much more enjoyable.

Effie said she had been keeping up with the events in Israel. Though not Jewish, she knew the history of the Jewish people and was empathetic toward our plight. She praised the efforts of the early immigrants who had prepared Palestine for future development. She even surprised me by recounting a personal experience with these pioneers! In her hometown of Thessaloniki, which was one of the main ports in Greece, she and her family had met several Jews who worked as longshoremen; these men explained that they were going to help build up the port of Haifa. Effie was

Israel, Effie, and I (bottom right) on deck

impressed by my work in importing and by my service in the military. She was very curious about the details of both.

We met almost daily after lunch, even if the seas were somewhat rough. Once, when it was raining, we hid behind the smokestacks. She kept hugging me and asking me to promise that I would make an effort to go to McGill. When she began kissing me, I managed to stay calm—although I was naturally excited by her display of affection. I explained that it wasn't the time or place to get too close.

I continued to spend time with Effie; I was glad to have the opportunity to get to know a young Greek lady who was beautiful and intelligent. I tried not to encourage her romantic interest, however; I knew the likelihood of my going to McGill was remote.

There were four classes of passengers on the *LaGuardia*. Of course, first class was the most luxurious grade of accommodation. The other three classes constituted steerage. (I was in fourth class.) Naturally, as the number *increased*, the quality of the lodgings and meals *decreased*. All steerage travelers were restricted to the third-class dining hall. We were not allowed to eat at the two onboard restaurants.

About five days before we were due to arrive in New York, I gave in to my curiosity and ventured into the upper-class sections of the ship. On one of the levels, I observed a man sitting in front of a box, inserting coins into it, and pulling a lever. I watched for about ten minutes, but nothing seemed to happen. Then, after a pull of the lever, I heard the clanging of coins exiting the machine into a metal bin. I couldn't control my desire to know about this pastime, so I approached the man.

"Excuse me, sir," I said. "What is this machine, and what does it do?"

The man smiled. "This is a slot machine. You put coins in this slot and pull this handle." He indicated the parts of the apparatus as he referred to them. Then he pointed to the glass in the middle and added, "The reels spin for a bit then stop. Sometimes you can win a lot of money. Sometimes you might not win anything at all."

"Fascinating! I have never seen anything like it," I said.

The man kindly offered me a couple of coins. "These are quarters," he explained. "They are worth twenty-five cents each. I have to leave now, but you should give it a try."

After he left, I closely examined the coins. They had dimensions similar to some of the Israeli coins in my pocket, which were of significantly lesser value. I decided to see if my Israeli coins would work in the machine. I deposited five of them and pulled the lever; the reels spun, but no money came out. I tried several more times, with the same result. But on my final attempt, a torrent of coins poured into the bin. I was elated!

When I returned to my cabin, I offered to exchange my quarters for my roommates' Israeli coins. I collected around fifty of them, since they were four to a quarter. The next afternoon, I returned to the slot machine with the Israeli currency. I played for a few minutes without any luck. On the last pull, however, the symbols on the reels aligned in my favor—three "bars." I netted about twenty dollars. I felt like a rich man!

All the students aboard the *LaGuardia* experienced great joy on January 17, 1950, when the ship entered New

Farewell party for the students on the LaGuardia, January 16, 1950. (I am standing to the left of the pole, near the back, behind Effie.

York Harbor and passed the Statue of Liberty. I recall that morning vividly. Seeing the Statue of Liberty brought tears to my eyes. I knew this was the start of achieving my goals and making my contribution to society. We danced and sang upon seeing the beautiful Lady of the Lamp. I was sad, however, when the moment came to hug Effie goodbye. We promised to keep in touch, and we did exchange letters for a while.

Chapter 14

A Real Texas Steak: My Welcome to America

MY MOTHER'S BROTHER, PESACH DUKSIN, lived in Queens with his wife, Eva, and their six-month-old son, Jack. Not knowing my way around New York, I took a taxi to his apartment; the ride cost all of my slot machine winnings. Uncle Pesach was still at work, so Eva and I chatted. She told me something I didn't know—that my mother had introduced them. As I mentioned earlier, my mother was an accomplished matchmaker!

Eva had been planning to travel from Tel Aviv to the United States when she met my mother, who thought she would be an excellent match for her brother. Pesach was getting older, and Eva was a few years older than he. The two got along very well. They soon married and moved to the United States, where my uncle found a job in the printing department of a Jewish newspaper. The position allowed him to take care of his family quite comfortably; they lived in a small, second-floor apartment with a kitchen, living room, and dining area. It was very similar to my parents' place in Tel Aviv.

When Uncle Pesach arrived home, he gave me a big hug and a kiss. He asked where I was going to school. When

I told him about Taft, he said, "Tufts! That's not too far—in Massachusetts! It's an excellent school."

I clarified: "Not Tufts, but Taft. It's a community college in California."

My aunt and uncle questioned my going three thousand miles away and suggested that I try to enter a New York university instead. I explained the excellent opportunity waiting for me in California, and they reluctantly gave up trying to persuade me.

We spent two days recalling memories of our lives in Palestine. My adorable little cousin Jack was just a baby, but he did warm up to me after I played with him a bit. Before I left, my uncle loaned me a few dollars for the trip to California. After promising to visit the family again soon, I bid them farewell.

Israel's cousin was driving from New York to Austin, to attend the University of Texas. He invited us to join him on the drive. We went through big cities, small towns, and farmland. Israel and I were feeling a bit homesick, and the beautiful sights of America lifted our spirits. We also felt encouraged when Israel's cousin proposed that we might be able to join him at the university.

He arranged for us to meet the dean of the Economics Department, who asked about our educational goals. The man became quite excited when I described the offer from Taft—the director there was a personal friend of his and a delightful gentleman, recently appointed to his position. The dean assured us that the promises made by his friend in California would be kept. He also said he would let him know that Israel would be joining me at the college. He added that the best way to get to our destination was to take a train to Bakersfield and then a Greyhound bus to Taft. We stayed overnight in Austin and left the next day.

On the train, I began composing a letter to my family about my adventures so far. A young woman in our car was having a beer. I noticed her watching me. After a few minutes, she said, "Am I already drunk? Or are you writing in the wrong direction?"

"I'm using Hebrew," I responded, "which is written from right to left."

"What language is that?" she asked. "And where are you from? You look strange."

I explained that we were from Israel. She had never heard of the country and wanted to know more about it. Through a lot of conversing, we were able to explain to her the history of Israel and Jerusalem. Hearing we were from the Holy Land, she said her parents would love to meet us. She invited us to stay overnight in El Paso, which was one of the stops on our route. We accepted.

The young woman's family was a typical Christian household of the Bible Belt. Enamored with the Holy Land, her parents greeted us warmly. Though unaware of current events in the region, they inquired eagerly about cities and sites they had read about in the Bible. For dinner, steak was served. Steak is not part of traditional Israeli cuisine, and I had never eaten it before. It was delicious! Toward the end of this delightful evening, Israel and I contemplated switching to a school in El Paso. Ultimately, however, we decided to stick to our original plan.

The next day, we hugged our hosts goodbye and promised to return. I did return to El Paso many years later, on a business trip with Joan, although I did not look up the woman or her family. From El Paso, Israel and I continued by train to Bakersfield. We arrived two days later, around noon, and found the bus station. We called the director of the college to say we were about to board a bus to Taft. With great hopes and high expectations, we headed out.

As the bus moved through the arid, flat, and desolate San Joaquin Valley, Israel startled me by nudging my arm. "Where's the beautiful paradise you told me about?" he grumbled. "Looks more like the Sinai. I wouldn't be surprised if we came across a caravan of Bedouins on camels. Guess you fell for Lillian's charms and her dreams of Shangri-la."

When we saw a sign that read "Taft City Limit," we rose from our seats. Forests of oil derricks flanked the road as we passed through an oil field. The pumps generated a deafening sound, and the crude oil emitted a foul odor. Discouraged, Israel growled, "A hell of a place to come to from the other side of the world."

As we entered the downtown area, the bus stopped at the Greyhound depot on Taft's main street. The late afternoon sun cast long, gloomy shadows across the shabby buildings. A few people wearing blue jeans and boots milled about. Aside from the paved street and parked cars, the dull scene was reminiscent of a town in the Old West.

Depressed by the view, I said, "I admit that I fell for Lillian's charms. Taft looks like a hole in the wall. Let's get out of here. LA is only 120 miles away. With luck, we can get there tonight."

"Okay," Israel replied. "It's not *entirely* your fault. You're gullible, but how about those letters from the director, promising . . ."

A loud, raspy voice interrupted him. The bus driver, anxious to get home, shouted, "Hey, fellas, this is the last stop, the end of the road. Scram! Get lost!"

We begged him to take us back to Bakersfield, and he told us to sit in the rear.

In our dejected state, we barely noticed a neatly dressed man get on the bus. He asked the driver if there were any students onboard. He replied, "No, only those two bums in the back." The way we were dressed, in old clothes and our army boots, we probably looked like derelicts. We were startled when the man addressed us in a deep, calm voice.

"You must be the two students from Israel," he began. "I am Mr. Cosand, the director of Taft College. Welcome to Taft—or should I say, 'Shalom!'? It's the only Hebrew word I have learned from my good old secretary, Elizabeth. She is a devout Catholic, and when she received your first letter, she almost wept. To have a student from the Holy Land at Taft College is a dream come true for her. I hope you brought her a rosary from Jerusalem. But we can discuss all this later."

Mr. Cosand helped us with our suitcases and led us to his car, a Cadillac. Once inside the vehicle, we were introduced to the driver; she was also a student at Taft. I'll call her Cindy, because I can't recall her actual name.

"This is your home away from home," Mr. Cosand announced as the car stopped at a wide building apart from the rest. "The semester starts next week, so you will have several days of peace before the other students arrive. It will be a good opportunity to get acquainted with the campus and its surroundings."

Mr. Cosand, Israel, and I exited the car and approached the building. Opening the dormitory doors, Mr. Cosand said, "Gentlemen, I hope you will enjoy your stay with us. The adjustment will not be easy, but you can count on my full support. You should know that I invited you here for reasons that you will discover in due course. Therefore, I feel a special responsibility for you. Your success or failure will also be mine."

With these ominous words, he led us to our room. "Freshen up now, relax, and Cindy will pick you up at seven to join my family for dinner." Extending his hand, he added, "Good luck and shalom," leaving us alone in our new home.

"Wow!" exclaimed Israel, giving me a jab in the side. "I don't care what you plan to do, but I'm staying. Did you get a good look at Cindy, and that car? Pinch me, I want to make sure I'm not dreaming!"

"Stop jumping like a Bedouin racing on his camel!" I chided him. "I also found Cindy attractive, and the car impressive, but what about that little speech? Why on earth did Mr. Cosand invite us here? And what did he mean by, 'Your success or failure will also be mine'? But *la-azazel*, what the devil, we are surely going to find out—because I intend to stay here, too. I am determined to get an education—dead or alive!"

Cindy came by promptly at seven and drove us to the Cosands' elaborate residence. After escorting us to the parlor, she studied our appearance and said, "You look like a pair of barbarians! You must come from an underdeveloped country. I wonder how you'll be received at school."

I responded, "Israel may not have the same luxuries as the United States, but we are very hardworking people and just went through an extremely difficult war. It will take time for the country to attain economic prosperity."

She asked what we wanted to drink, and we both requested Coca-Cola. Mr. Cosand then entered with his wife and introduced us to her. She welcomed us with a smile.

"I have read a lot about Israel and your people's accomplishments," she said. "I hope you will have a pleasant time at school and in our little community," she added. Then we sat down for dinner.

Israel and I were on either side of Cindy, who watched us struggle to figure out how to use each piece of silverware correctly. At home, we had only a knife, a spoon, and a fork, so there was nothing to be confused about! Here, there were several different forks and spoons at each place, and we didn't know which to use first.

"This proves it!" Cindy muttered. "You *are* barbarians. Let me show you!" She picked up the three forks in front of her and indicated which one was for the salad, which for the main course, and which for the dessert. She did the same with the various spoons. We got through the meal with some effort and only a few mistakes.

Unlike Cindy, Mr. and Mrs. Cosand were very gracious. They asked us many questions about the recent war and our participation in it. They wondered about our family life and told us more about Taft and its residents. After dinner, Mr. Cosand gave us a quick tour of the campus and drove us back to the dorm. He told us more about the college and the teachers with whom we would studying. He had informed them about us and was certain they would be very welcoming.

Chapter 15

Lunch on the House: A Celebrity in Taft, California

I WASN'T SURE how well I would fit in or make friends at Taft, but I hoped for the best. As the semester was about to start, students began to move into the dorm. One of them was John—Lillian's GI boyfriend. He heard I had arrived and found me in my room one evening. Israel and I introduced ourselves to him.

"Welcome!" he said, giving each of us a hug. "I'm glad you took Lillian's advice! I just finished my term in the service, and I'm here on the GI Bill. I heard you served in the military in Israel. I'd be interested to find out what that was like."

"I'd be happy to share my experiences with you," I replied. And that was how our friendship began.

Making friends came naturally to me. Succeeding academically was another matter. Economics and geology were my most challenging subjects. My economics teacher provided the students with a textbook and a weekly subscription to TIME Magazine, so we could keep up with current events. The problem was the unfamiliar terminology; I was always looking up the meanings of words. In my geology class, the discussion often focused on a place I didn't know—the Grand Canyon.

My trouble with French was of a different nature. The class was predominantly female, and some of the girls were bewildered by my attire; they would giggle amongst themselves when they saw me wearing shorts in the middle of winter. Israel received the same treatment in one of his classes. We decided to wear our military slacks from then on, though that didn't really help. Overall, however, both the teachers and the students were quite friendly.

John and I discussed the difficulties I was having with my studies, and he made me a proposition. "I love Lillian and need to learn more about her religion. If you'd be willing to teach me about the Old Testament and Israel, I could help you understand your economics coursework. I'd be your personal dictionary!"

The terms seemed agreeable to me. "I accept your offer!" I said with a smile. We shook hands.

The first weekend of the semester, John invited me to a local restaurant for lunch. It was owned by a deeply religious woman, who greeted us and showed us to our table. John introduced me.

"This is my friend Shami," he said. "He's from Israel. He arrived in Taft just recently."

"You're from Israel? You lived in Jerusalem?" she asked in disbelief. "I'm delighted to meet you! This is such an honor! Lunch is on the house today, as my welcome gift to you! Order anything you like, and I'll even prepare a special dessert for you!"

After John and I finished our meal, the woman promptly brought out an ice cream sundae—a first for me. She started to walk back to the kitchen but turned around and approached the table again. "Shami, I've been thinking about something for the last half hour. I've always dreamed of getting a rosary from the Holy Land. Might you have one on you? Even if I could just look at it, I'd be so happy."

I remembered that the rosaries I had bought in Italy were from the Holy Land. "You know, I do happen to have one." I pulled it from my pocket and showed it to her. She admired it as though it were the greatest work of art, afraid to touch it and in absolute awe.

"I know you may not be willing to part with it, but maybe you would let me hold it."

The woman had no idea I was Jewish and that rosaries didn't matter to me. I knew the string of beads would mean much more to her than it ever would to me, and I had purchased it to give as a gift anyway, so I made a decision.

"It would be my pleasure to give you this rosary, in appreciation of your kind hospitality."

"Thank you, thank you!" she cried. She leaned down and kissed my cheek. "You don't know how happy you've made me!" She shook my hand vigorously before giving me a big hug. "Come here any day, for lunch or dinner, and you'll be my guests for the entire semester."

I had not foreseen how remarkable an asset those rosaries would be!

One Sunday afternoon, John invited me to visit Bakersfield with him. After a short tour of the city, he took me to a special gathering of young people at a nightclub. "You should experience more aspects of the Wild West," he told me. It was a strip joint! I had never even heard of such an establishment. I was particularly struck by the actions of the young men, calling the women over so they could place dollar bills in their skimpy outfits.

"OUR TOWN"

COUGAR ECHO

TONIGHT 8:15

VOL. 1—NO. 1 TAFT, CALIFORNIA FRIDAY, FEBRUARY 17, 1950

RECENT ARRIVALS

Two new students from Tel Aviv have recently arrived in Taft. They are Israel Shafir and Samuel Rimmon.

Israel is taking a pre-med course and expects to stay in the United States for four years and then return to Tel Aviv to attend the graduate school there. Samuel will major in economics and expects to return to Tel Aviv, also.

It's been three years since Israel has studied, but he can speak Hebrew, Jewish, Polish and German. besides English.

Israel has been employed as a librarian in the Central Library in Tel Aviv and was in the Israeli Army for a few months. With respect to the food and political situation here, Israel thinks it is very pleasant.

The Israel government allows only a limited amount of dollars to go out of the country; only recommended students are permitted to study abroad.

Israel and Samuel learned of Taft Junior College from Miss Lillian Frank. Miss Frank is expected to arrive soon in Taft, She was born in Germany, went to China and to Tel Aviv.

Rimmon corresponded with Dean Cosand about the junior college. On the ship with Samuel and Israel were several other students from Tel Aviv. They seemed very interested in accounts of Taft Junior College.

Most of these students are destined for the University of California at Berkeley. Tuition fees there will take about half the amount they were allowed to bring.

When the two became interested in Taft, they made plans with two other friends who are still in the army. They expect their friends to come to the United States and to Taft when they are released.

Israel and Samuel live in the old dormitory; so many of you fellows probably have met them. On behalf of the rest of the student body, welcome to Taft Junior College.

An article in the Taft College newspaper, the Cougar Echo

Daily Midway Driller

THE HOME NEWSPAPER FOR THE WEST SIDE

TAFT, CALIFORNIA, WEDNESDAY, FEBRUARY 15, 1950

Freedom To Trust Found By Students

By Edith Dane

"It's a small world!"

A trite expression, but certainly applicable to the story of the latest foreign students in Taft Junior College, and how they learned of our school. This story is of a girl in far-off Shanghai, who was told of the Taft school by some homesick boy during the war. The magic tale of free education in a land of kindly people remained with her all the way across the great continent of Asia (we hope to hear that story some day) to Tel Aviv, where she told it to two young men, Samuel Rimmon and Izrail Szafir.

The story entranced these two young men. They investigated and started on the weary road of applications, qualifications, permits, and all the red tape which, finally unwound, led them to Taft about two weeks ago. The girl is hoping to finally unroll enough of the same red tape to lead her to Taft.

The boys express themselves as delighted with the school and the warm-heartedness of students and faculty, though Samuel Rimmon says there were times when he wondered if they were chasing a will-o-the-wisp, when he asked people in New York City about Taft Junior College, and no one seemed to have heard of it.

It's interesting to see the foreign students relax and lose most of their formailty after a very few weeks's association with our easy western ways. One thing that seems to make an impression above all else on these newcomers to our community, one which they all speak of, could be called, I think, "The Freedom to Trust."

An article in the local Taft newspaper, the Daily Midway Driller

Israeli Students Follow Orient Tip to Taft J.C.

Because a Taft G.I. visited Shanghai, two Israeli students enrolled at Taft Junior College two weeks ago.

Samuel Rimmon, 25, and Israel Szafir, 21, both Israeli air force veterans of the recent strife in the Holy Land, left their parents in Tel Aviv a month ago, bound for Kern county.

They were part of a group of 30 ex-servicemen granted permission from the Israeli government to study in the United States. The students paid their own fare and must continue to support themselves during their schooling. Their homeland is on the pound sterling and the drop of its exchange value to $2.80 "froze" the exporting of funds.

Most of the tanned young veterans enrolled in San Mateo Junior College or the University of California at Berkeley. Rimmon and Szafir selected Taft because "a girl we met from Shanghai heard so much about it from an American G.I.," Rimmon said.

Wilderness Hub

"No one knew of Taft in Israel. We expected it to be in the middle of a wilderness," the spokesman of the duo explained. He expected to find the wild west of the movies but, then, he finds most Taft students have a similarly erroneous impression of modern Tel Aviv.

Located on the Mediterranean coast, the "most overcrowded city in the world" has a fast-growing population of 300,000. Downtown there are crowded department sotres, lineups for American movies and hundreds waiting to enter the restaurants, he said.

The proportionate number of cars per family is far under the figure in this nation, and the modern buses can't begin to cope with the queues at every bus stop, even in the residential areas.

The youths speak English with a marked accent, being more familiar with Hebrew and Yiddish. English and Hebrew are languages on the compulsory list for each Israeli student from grade school to university.

Swallowed by Russia

Rimmon was born in Vilna, Lithuania, a country which has since been swallowed up by Russia. Szafir is a native of Warsaw, Poland, also under present Russian domination. Both youths had their schooling in the Zionist-settled land of Palestine.

World War II found Rimmon enrolled in the "Hagannah," the small force of patriots that took militant action to gain a Jewish state. In 1948 he joined the regular Israeli army and became a staff sergeant (samal tayis). He met Private Szafir, recently out of school, following the partitioning of Palestine by the United Nations.

A letter to J. P. Cosand, dean of Taft Junior College, brought a reply that the West Side would be pleased to enroll the Mediterranean students. Rimmon is majoring in economics and Szafir is studying a pre-medical course. They "get along fine" with their fellow students, and expressed pleasure at the friendly, informal manner of Taftians.

Complex Chore

There will be a lot of midnight oil burned by the visitors that live in the college dormitory. They can't grasp the unfamiliar English technical words as fast as the native students and taking notes becomes more than the usual chore.

The boys aren't nearly as worried about the course as they are about funds. To augment their small reserve, Rimmon and Szafir plan to start an adult course in teaching Hebrew. They plan to be in Bakersfield each week end to instruct a Hebrew class at B'nai Jacob Synagogue, open to any interested linguist or Biblical student.

Above and right: an article in the Bakersfield newspaper, the Bakersfield Californian

FOLLOW SHANGHAI TIP—Two students with a thirst for knowledge, are taking courses in Taft Junior College. They were drawn to the West Side Kern county school after hearing about the friendly California town from a girl that had been in Shanghai. A GI there had done a little community boosting and thus the word "got around." The two young men pictured here (left to right right) are Samuel Rimmon and Israel Szafir.

The second week of the semester, Mr. Cosand called me into his office to disclose why he had offered me privileges and incentives to come to Taft. A progressive man, he felt that the student body was too homogenous; he wanted to bring in foreign students to create more diversity. My letter, therefore, had arrived at a very opportune time. Furthermore, Mr. Cosand believed that inviting a Jew from the Holy Land was a kind thing to do.

He also informed me that Cindy, the driver from my first day in Taft, wanted to interview me for the school newspaper. Cindy and I set a time to meet. When I showed up, she greeted me with a genuine smile. She seemed friendlier than at the dinner with Mr. and Mrs. Cosand. First, she had a "big question" for me.

"What are your hobbies?" she asked.

"I'm sorry, I'm not familiar with that term," I said. "What does it mean?"

"Hobbies are the things you do when you aren't working or studying," she explained. "They're the things you do for fun."

I wanted to impress her, so I said, "I listen to classical music, and I read books and poetry."

She laughed. "Do you play any games?"

"Yes, chess," I replied.

She looked perplexed, as if I were from another planet. "That seems, you know, kind of boring. Don't you do anything *fun*?" she pursued.

Feeling a little rebuffed, I turned the question on her. "What are *your* hobbies?"

"Bowling, jitterbugging, and necking," she answered.

"I have no idea what those are, but they sound interesting," I said.

"Tell you what—I'll teach you all of them, and report about your progress in the paper." I wasn't sure I wanted her to publicize that information.

The conversation turned more serious when Cindy asked me about my family, my life in Israel, and my military service. She preferred to keep things light, however, so we soon concluded the exchange. Cindy interviewed Israel for the story, as well.

The article that appeared in the paper focused mainly on how Israel and I arrived at Taft. It didn't refer to my hobbies—though I was looking forward to learning about Cindy's.

In addition to the *Cougar Echo*, the Taft and Bakersfield newspapers interviewed Israel and me. Since we didn't get to review the pieces before they were published, some of the details were exaggerated or not exactly as we had told the reporters. In fact, each article spelled Israel's name differently! (I was referred to as "Samuel," the name used in my school records.) The multiple articles gave us wider recognition on campus, augmenting our circle of friends.

Chapter 16

Salamis in the Mail: Looking for My Community

AFTER OUR FIRST WEEK IN TAFT, Israel and I began to feel the lack of a Jewish community. One Friday afternoon, John volunteered to take us to Bakersfield so we could attend a Shabbat evening service. We would stay at a motel near the synagogue, and John would pick us up on Sunday to take us back to school.

Israel and I were kindly welcomed by the gabbai, the official in charge of running the services at the synagogue. After the service, he invited us to a reception with several congregants. When we told them we were from Israel and attending Taft College, they cried out, "Taft? That's the last place you should study. There are no Jews there, and you will have no Jewish life."

One man invited us to his home for lunch the next day. The house was lovely, in a very nice section of Bakersfield. Several members of the synagogue's board were there, too. After questioning us about Israel, they tried to convince us to study in Bakersfield. They offered us work and help with the cost of school, but we told them we couldn't break our agreement with Taft's director. So they made us an offer we did accept: to teach Hebrew at their Shabbat school every weekend, for a nice compensation.

After lunch, one of the guests invited us to his home and introduced us to his daughter, who was about twenty. She was congenial but not someone in whom Israel or I had a romantic interest (if that had been her father's hope). She took us on a walking tour of Bakersfield, explaining that her parents owned a cattle farm and hinting that they were very well-off. Along the way, we stopped by the house of a friend of hers; Israel took an immediate liking to the young woman, but I had Cindy's promise to teach me her hobbies on my mind.

For the first month, John would drop us off in Bakersfield on Fridays and pick us up on Sundays. Then Israel and I pooled our money and bought a very old used car, which served to transport us to and from Bakersfield, and around Taft. For almost the entire semester, we spent our weekends in Bakersfield and saved our earnings.

I settled into campus life. I went to classes, improved my English, and developed relationships with other students. After three weeks, the Rotary Club of Bakersfield invited Israel and me to a luncheon, to give a talk on the Israeli War of Independence. (The Rotary Club is an international service organization made up of business and professional leaders.) When we arrived at the event, I was really impressed that they had ordered kosher food from Los Angeles especially for us. In broken English, we tried our best to explain the dangers we experienced in the war, being attacked by neighboring nations.

During a pause, a voice from the audience called out, "The surrounding countries were larger and better equipped. Wasn't it a miracle that Israel won?"

"Our success was not a miracle," I replied. "We won due to our intense preparation and training. The Haganah, which was a paramilitary organization, had us learn every part of our country, no matter how small or remote. This knowledge gave us an invaluable advantage. We also made any sacrifices necessary to save our families, our homes, and our land. We had no other choice. If we failed, we would find ourselves drowning in the Mediterranean Sea. We couldn't fail." My final statement was met with applause and a standing ovation. After the talk, Rotary members approached us, asked us questions, thanked us for coming, and invited us to visit the club anytime.

Before I left for the United States, my father had told me about his cousin Ben Solnit, who lived in Los Angeles. I sent Ben a letter to let him know I had arrived safely in California. When we spoke later on the phone, I described my studies at Taft and my work in Bakersfield. Ben was pleased with my accomplishments but emphatic that I would be better off in Los Angeles. He even invited me to stay with him until I could find a place to live. I assured him that my situation was satisfactory for the present.

Concerned about the lack of Jewish cuisine in Taft, Ben often sent me large kosher salamis in the mail. But his efforts to feed me were futile! When one of those packages arrived, my dorm-mates would line up at my door with cans of beer, awaiting my return from class. As soon as I invited my pals to have a taste, they would demolish the salami, leaving not a bite for me! Ben's tasty gifts did, however, earn me the appreciation of many.

During the first month or so in Taft, Cindy taught me how to jitterbug, bowl, and golf. But she wasn't the only young lady with whom I spent my time. Laura, a lovely girl in my French class and a native of Taft, invited me to a barbecue at her parents' house during a school holiday. Unlike my visit to the Rotary Club in Bakersfield, this gathering did not focus on my identity as a Jew from Israel. Laura's parents didn't flood me with questions; instead, they offered me a beer and invited me to join their family and friends in the backyard. The food was superb. We discussed politics in Taft and the state of the world. Occasionally, someone would inquire about Israel.

After the meal, everyone sat down and played cards. Laura attempted to teach me a version of poker that was different than the one my uncle had taught me in Petach Tikvah. At the time, I preferred playing chess, but Laura, like Cindy, thought maneuvering pieces around a chessboard was boring. Laura introduced me to several of her friends; in the process of visiting their homes, I learned that the locals were friendly and welcoming. I also discovered that most of the residents of Taft and the surrounding communities were involved in the oil business.

The people of this small American community knew basically nothing about Israel or Judaism. They were satisfied with their lives and had little interest in global affairs or the Middle East. The only Jewish family in town owned a store and were not open about their religious identity. To some extent, being in Taft and Bakersfield gave me a sense of life on the American frontier! The men wore jeans, cowboy boots, and cowboy hats; the women dressed in frilly Western outfits. I recognized their attire from the few Westerns I had seen back in Israel.

Laura took me to the oil fields, where I met some of the workers. They explained to me the details of oil production and the complex jobs they performed. I encountered pumpers, drillers, riggers, machinists, and a type of worker I had never heard of—"roustabouts." These unskilled laborers carried out various challenging and even dangerous tasks in the oil fields; their job was dirty but well-paid. I found the oil industry fascinating—despite the stench. I appreciated the livelihood it provided for the communities in and around Taft and the support it gave to the college.

Laura began hinting that she was interested in more than a friendship with me, mentioning that she loved family life,

At an oil field in Taft, March 1950

children, and the comfortable existence in Taft. She encouraged me to continue my studies there and to visit her more often. But my goals reached far beyond Taft College, particularly since Ben kept urging me to come to Los Angeles. He would try to help me get into UCLA, which offered many more learning opportunities than Taft. Furthermore, my friends in Bakersfield warned me that staying in Taft would not be wise.

One weekend, when Israel and I were having lunch with a family in Bakersfield, I was introduced to Jill, the niece of our host. Jill lived in Los Angeles. She took me aside to tell me about her school, Los Angeles City College. Located close to the Jewish community on Vermont Avenue, LACC had many Jewish students, lots of available classes, excellent instructors, and—best of all—low tuition fees. Jill offered to

With Laura, March 1950

TAFT JUNIOR COLLEGE SEMESTER REPORT CARD

Samuel Rimmon .... Sem. 2, 1949-1950

NAME OF STUDENT

SIGNIFICANCE OF MARK
A—Excellent
B—Good
C—Average
D—Barely Passed
E—Incomplete
F—Failed
W—Withdrawn

SUBJECTS	UNITS	MARKS
English 1B	3	B
French 2	4	B
Economics 1B	3	B
Geology 1B	3	B
History 4B	3	B

OFFICE OF THE DEAN
Taft Junior College
TAFT, CALIFORNIA

EB .... SIGNATURE

6-12-50 .... DATE

My report card from Taft College, June 1950

give me a tour of the campus when I visited LA. Until then, we agreed to keep in touch by mail. That evening, Jill took me to a drive-in, where we saw a film starring Ginger Rogers and Fred Astaire. I wasn't able to concentrate on the movie, however, because Jill was somewhat amorous.

During our weekly trips to Bakersfield, Israel and I had many discussions. We agreed that since we both had relatives in Los Angeles, we should continue our education there. Toward the end of the semester, I requested a meeting with Mr. Cosand. I told him that Israel and I had enjoyed our classes very much and were deeply grateful for his support, but we both had family members in Los Angeles who wanted to help us get into UCLA. He graciously accepted our choice and wished us success.

My six months in Taft gave me a wonderful introduction to America. Despite my inadequate English, I managed to earn Bs in all my classes and accumulate sixteen

With my Nash, June 1950

undergraduate units. I was very satisfied with my efforts and pleased with the opportunities these good marks would afford me. When I received my grades, I felt that I had taken an important step toward my dream of attending a university.

In June 1950, I said farewell to Mr. and Mrs. Cosand, Cindy, Laura, and the rest of my friends in Taft. Israel bought my share of the car. I used the money, along with my earnings, to purchase a 1939 Nash. Israel and I promised to stay in touch. Eventually, we would both realize our shared goal of attending UCLA. We remained friends until graduation but lost contact after he married his cousin in Los Angeles.

On my way out of the San Joaquin Valley, I stopped in Bakersfield to say goodbye to my acquaintances there. I thanked them for their friendship and assistance over the past few months. As I reflected on my interesting experiences in Taft and Bakersfield, I felt a bit sad to be leaving.

Chapter 17

Cucumbers and Tomatoes: Feeling at Home in Los Angeles

ON THE THREE-HOUR DRIVE from Bakersfield to Los Angeles in my old jalopy, I contemplated the possibilities awaiting me. Once again, I was schlepping my metal suitcase, containing all of my possessions, to a new destination. My cousin Ben had offered me a room in his house while I looked for permanent lodgings. It was evening by the time I reached Sunset and Doheny, in West Hollywood. Ben lived on Oriole Drive, at the top of a steep incline in the Hollywood Hills. Thankfully, the Nash was able to make the climb.

Upon exiting the car, I was overwhelmed by the view of the city. Ben and his wife, Bertha, greeted me. They introduced me to their daughters, June and Mary, and to their daughters' husbands, Sam and Ben. During a homey family meal, we discussed our relatives in Israel, my stint in the military, and my experiences in Taft and Bakersfield. Ben reiterated that coming to Los Angeles was a positive move for my education.

Over the next few days, June and Mary invited me to their homes, which were still higher on the mountain. We took a ride on Mulholland Drive, and the view was even more impressive than from Ben's house; I could see all the way from Downtown Los Angeles to the Pacific Ocean.

Ben was amazed by my old Nash. One day, he suggested we take it out. We drove down Doheny to Sunset, and there, in the middle of the intersection, the car stopped! We created a minor traffic jam, and the other vehicles started honking at us. Ben's amazement quickly turned to fury.

"I have never been so embarrassed in all my life!" he bellowed. "Where on earth did you find this piece of junk?"

I tried everything I could to restart the car, but nothing worked. A few men in nearby cars tried to help us push it, but it seemed welded to the earth. Ben called the Automobile Club to tow it to a nearby repair shop. There, the mechanic diagnosed the problem right away.

"Which one of you is the owner?" he asked.

I nodded as Ben excused himself to make a phone call. The mechanic proceeded.

"Son, you've got yourself quite, uh, an antique vehicle. I haven't seen a car like this in years!" I chuckled, and he smiled. He continued, "Part of your car has fallen clean out! It must have been wedged underneath the engine. I can have it fixed by tomorrow. It'll cost you eighty dollars."

I agreed. Just then, Ben returned and announced that one of his daughters was on her way to get us. Back at the house, we decided to go for a ride in Ben's Cadillac instead.

The day after my car was repaired, I called Jill, the LACC student I had met in Bakersfield. We agreed to meet, and she gave me directions to her house. When I arrived, she immediately questioned me about my car.

"What on earth is that?" she asked, not disguising her disgust.

"My car," I said. "It's a Nash."

"Looks like a piece of junk to me," she observed. "Doesn't look like it could go anywhere!"

"Believe it or not, it brought me here from Taft," I affirmed. "And it has served me well."

She continued to stare at the Nash, puzzled. "Let's take my car," she finally suggested. "I know how to get where we're going."

Off we went to a local coffee shop. After we placed our order, she asked me about my housing situation.

"I'm living with a cousin and his family," I told her, "but I don't want to stay there too long. His daughters' husbands work in the family business and are in and out of the house quite often. I need a calmer environment."

"I know a family that's looking for a boarder," she said. "They live off of Vermont. Good people. Slower pace. And it's only about two miles from LACC. Speaking of which, have you enrolled?"

"Not yet," I said, regretting that I hadn't done so.

"Well, what are you waiting for? Let's do it right now!"

We finished our drinks and drove to Los Angeles City College. We parked on a nearby street and walked over to the admissions office. I showed the woman there my report card from Taft. She said, "Looks like you're a pretty good student. I can't see any reason why you wouldn't be successful here. Let's get you enrolled."

I filled out some forms, which she processed immediately. And just like that, I was enrolled! The woman told me about tuition and other student fees, which were reasonable; I knew I could manage the cost if I had a job.

"Let's celebrate!" I told Jill after our business at the admissions office was completed. "Pick any restaurant you want." When we were in Bakersfield, Jill had promised to give me a tour of the campus, but there wasn't time that day.

She chose a Chinese place. I had never had Chinese food before, so the experience was memorable. The dishes were so different from Jewish cooking and what I had eaten in Taft. Jill then drove us back to her house. We agreed to get together again the following week.

The next day, I called the family Jill had mentioned; they agreed to meet me right away. I drove to their house, which was at 849 South Berendo Street. When I knocked on the door, Jacob and Sally Nidelman invited me in and introduced me to their daughters, Rebecca and Sarah.

"Jill recommended you very highly," Sally said. "She told us about some of your accomplishments in Israel. Such an interesting background! We would be very glad to have you as a tenant."

Rebecca stepped forward to give me a tour. First, she led me to the room that would be mine. It was modest, containing a bed and a writing desk. The walls were decorated with nicely framed paintings. One depicted the Israeli president, Chaim Weizmann; another showed the American president, Harry Truman. The rest of the pictures were of flowers. The room's windows faced the street, offering a glimpse of the small neighboring houses. Next, Rebecca showed me the bathroom, which everyone shared. Then I saw the other two bedrooms and the kitchen, which had a small dining area. Finally, we returned to the living room, which was close to the front door.

"Jill probably told you that your room and board will be $150 per month," Jacob said.

"Yes," I replied, "and I will pay you the first of the month."

"Excellent," he said. "We'll let you unpack and settle in. When it's time for dinner, we'll let you know."

I went to my room, where I arranged my things and rested. I was pleased to have found a nice family to stay with, in a convenient location. A little later, Rebecca came to announce that dinner was ready. As Sally and Rebecca served the meal, the small talk commenced.

"Like you, we are Jewish," Jacob began. "We observe the Jewish traditions. We share Friday evening Shabbat meals, and I usually pray in the morning before work. Sally manages the household. Sarah attends UCLA, and Rebecca works with me in the garment district, as a secretary. May I ask what languages you speak?"

"Hebrew and Yiddish," I replied.

"Wonderful!" he exclaimed. "If you learn any secrets from my daughters, you can tell me in Yiddish. And if you hear anything from my wife, you can tell me in Hebrew!" He gave me a playful nudge.

"I'm not one for divulging secrets, sir, but I would enjoy speaking with you in either Hebrew or Yiddish. Since I left Israel, I have conversed in Hebrew only with my friend Israel. It would be good practice for me." I was curious about his daughters, both of whom were very attractive, but I decided to be patient.

Dinner reminded me of the meals I'd had with my family on Shenkin Street in Tel Aviv. It consisted of chicken, cucumbers and tomatoes, and bread, accompanied by tea and apple slices.

"I understand you plan to study at LA City College," Sally said. "It's not far from here, maybe fifteen minutes. Do you have a car?"

"Yes, ma'am, I do. It's a Nash. It's parked on the street."

"I'm not familiar with that type of car. You'll have to let me take a look sometime."

"LACC is a very nice school," Rebecca chimed in. "I went there before transferring to UCLA. If you'd like, I can give you a tour."

"That would be wonderful," I replied. "On another topic, I'm looking for a job. In Bakersfield, I tutored children in Hebrew on the weekends. Are there any synagogues in the area where I might find similar work?"

"Try the one we go to," Jacob recommended. "It's a twenty-minute drive." He turned to Rebecca. "Can you take him there after you visit the college?"

"Yes, I can," she said. She looked at me and added, "I'll introduce you to the rabbi, so you can talk with him."

"That's very kind," I replied. I said to Sally, "Thank you for dinner. This meal reminded me of home." Then I addressed the table: "I am very pleased to be part of your extended family. I hope you all have a pleasant evening. I'm going to do some reading now. I'll see you in the morning." As I excused myself, I said to Jacob, "*Toda raba*" (thank you very much). He smiled and said, "*Laila tov*" (good night).

Before retiring to my room, I called Ben to let him know I had found a place to stay. He congratulated me on my swift progress and wished me well.

The next day, Rebecca saw my car and suggested that we take hers. (I was getting used to this reaction.) When we arrived at LACC in her shiny red Chevy, we looked at several buildings, including an auditorium and a recreational facility. The campus appeared older and more worn than Taft but otherwise not much different. Then we headed to the synagogue, which was four or five miles away. "I told you I would introduce you to the rabbi," Rebecca reminded me.

After thanking her, I asked, "Why are you being so kind to me? You don't have to be. I'm only a tenant."

With a subtly suggestive expression, she replied, "You look like a nice young man. I want to help you as much as possible."

We arrived at the synagogue, Congregation Knesseth Israel of Hollywood, which seemed recently built. The secretary explained that the rabbi was in a meeting with a parent, and we would have to wait a few minutes. Rebecca and I sat down in the lobby.

"My parents attend this synagogue regularly," she said. "My sister and I come only during the holidays. Getting a job here would be very convenient for you, because it's close to school and to the apartment. But if you don't, I'll help you find work somewhere else."

I thanked Rebecca again for her kindness. About twenty minutes later, I was called in to meet the rabbi. He greeted me with a friendly shalom.

"Please tell me, how I can help you?" he inquired.

"Rabbi, I arrived in Los Angeles only a few days ago," I started. "Before that, I studied at Taft College. I plan to continue my education at LA City College. I came to the United States after completing my military service in Israel. Right now, I'm looking for a job. I can work evenings and weekends. Do you have a need for a bar mitzvah tutor or a Sunday school teacher? While I was in Taft, I taught at a synagogue in Bakersfield."

The rabbi looked perplexed. "Tufts is not in California. It's in Massachusetts!"

Again, I explained that the school wasn't *Tufts* but *Taft*, which was located about forty miles (sixty-four kilometers) southwest of Bakersfield.

"Well, it's very easy to be confused! You must have a good work ethic, to drive so far for a job. How did you like teaching?"

"I enjoyed it, but I had to leave in order to pursue other opportunities. The rabbi was sad to see me go, but he understood and wished me well."

"Tell me a bit about your life in Israel," he requested.

I spent fifteen minutes describing my studies, my work, and my military service.

"You have achieved quite a lot. I have good news for you. We can use a person with your experience to tutor for bar mitzvah and to teach both Sunday and Saturday—but only after the summer and High Holidays." (He was referring to the Jewish festivals of Rosh Hashanah and Yom Kippur.) "This synagogue is relatively new, and our budget is tight. Nevertheless, I will provide you with a reasonable salary."

"Thank you very much for this opportunity," I said.

"I look forward to learning more about you," he concluded.

I shook his hand, and with a warm shalom, departed.

"How did it go?" Rebecca inquired as soon as she saw me.

"He hired me, but only after the High Holidays. Now I need to find a job for the summer."

We went to a small restaurant across from the college, where students gathered at lunchtime. Rebecca offered to pay for the meal, but I refused.

"It's my treat," I insisted.

"But you don't have much money!" she protested.

"I want to spend the little I have on a nice person," I assured her.

She gave me an amorous hug. I was baffled by her display of affection but decided not to make the situation awkward by objecting. My philosophy at the moment was *qué será, será* ("whatever will be, will be").

Chapter 18

Grape Juice and Challah: Shabbat at Big Bear Lake

WHEN REBECCA AND I RETURNED HOME from visiting the college and the synagogue, I retired to my room. I wrote letters to my family and friends in Israel. Then I called Ben.

"I need to find work right away, to cover my living expenses," I told him. "Can you help me find a summer job?"

Ben arranged for me to meet the director of the Hollywood Los Feliz Jewish Community Center, who happily gave me a job as a counselor at the center's summer day camp. It was called Camp JCA (Jewish Centers Association), or Camp JCA Shalom today. The director was particularly pleased to have me teach the children Hebrew and conduct the Friday afternoon pre-Shabbat services. The camp met in Griffith Park, a large city park located at the eastern end of the Santa Monica Mountains. The activities at the camp included horseback riding and baseball. I had been on the back end of a donkey before, but my contact with horses was nil. And I really didn't know anything about baseball. This job would be a real learning experience.

Several unexpected events occurred in the first month at camp. We had gone on an overnight excursion, and one of the campers got lost in the park. I alerted the director, and

At the Griffith Park horse stables (far right), summer 1950

he notified the boy's parents; of course, they were incredibly upset. The director also contacted the police. Together, we searched for the child. Within several hours, around midnight, a police officer found the youngster sleeping close to the observatory, a popular tourist attraction in the park. That weekend, several of the other counselors and I went to the boy's home to apologize for the incident.

The father said to me, "The experience was very shocking, but it wasn't your fault. Our son likes to explore and go off in different directions. Once, we even found him wandering on the golf course."

Our camp was adjacent to the golf course in the park. On another occasion, several campers disappeared from the campsite and were hiding on the green. A couple of golfers brought them back, complaining bitterly that the kids had interrupted their game. Naturally, I was concerned that

With my campers in Griffith Park, summer 1950

these incidents might lead to my termination. I went to the director and expressed my doubts about being allowed to work for the next camp session.

"Shmuel, I know you ran all over the place, looking for that boy alongside the police. These things happen sometimes. It isn't always controllable," he assured me. "I've heard about the fine job you've done with the children—in particular, with your Hebrew instruction and your stories about Israel. I understand that you introduced the game of soccer, which the children enjoyed. Would you be willing to continue working next month, as assistant head counselor? We have a ten-day camping trip planned at Big Bear Lake."

Relieved to hear praise instead of criticism, I accepted the position.

We met at the Jewish center and boarded buses for the drive to Big Bear. The road ran through a forest and up a mountain, to the lake. The campsite was next to the water; it had cabins and small rowboats.

Every morning at six, we awoke to a song being played over the loudspeaker: "Oh What a Beautiful Mornin'," from the Broadway musical *Oklahoma!* With no covering above us except the leaves of the trees, our prayers during the day seemed to go directly to heaven. We had brought our own food, since there was nowhere to purchase kosher items at the lake. Our activities were very similar to those at other camps, except at night, when we sat around the fire, instead of ghost stories, I told stories about life in Israel. I told the campers that Big Bear Lake reminded me of Israel's Lake Kinneret, also known as the Sea of Galilee; located in valleys and surrounded by mountains and forests, both bodies of water were very picturesque. The few evenings we had full moonlight, we took the rowboats out for a ride. "Lights out" for the campers was at 10:00 p.m.

After the campers went to sleep, some of the counselors remained on duty to provide supervision and security, while the others rowed out to the middle of the lake to visit with the female counselors from the girls' camp across the water. We had met some of them during shopping trips in the village nearby. A girl from one of their boats would get into the boat with one of our counselors, and vice versa. These rendezvous lasted a couple of hours; then we went back to our respective camps.

We celebrated Friday afternoon and evening with services and a Shabbat dinner, which included grape juice and challah. After the meal, we sang songs, and the campers shared stories about their bar mitzvahs.

On Shabbat morning, we got to sleep a little later and were not awakened by the loudspeaker. Prayer service began at eight o'clock, followed by breakfast, sports, a Shabbat lunch, and free time in the afternoon. We took hikes around the lake and in the forest. At nightfall, we held the Havdalah, the religious service marking the end of the Sabbath. The Havdalah involves lighting a special candle; because of the fire danger, we conducted the ceremony on the lakeshore, rather than among the trees.

Being a camp counselor gave me the opportunity to make many friends, both male and female. The other counselors clued me in on the city's social scene, including concerts, sports, and other forms of entertainment. Most of them seemed to be from middle class families, although some were wealthier. Several invited me to their homes. The majority lived in nice houses, including some posh residences in Beverly Hills. I learned a lot about young people in the United States. They seemed to have little interest in world affairs, including the newly established State of Israel. They were more involved in their daily lives, their studies, and having fun. A couple of the counselors attended LACC, and I looked forward to seeing them on campus.

After camp ended, I had three weeks to myself before the semester started. First, I visited Ben's brother, Harry Solnit, who lived in the Los Angeles neighborhood of Boyle Heights. At the time, Boyle Heights still had a thriving Jewish community; eventually, most of the Jews moved to the Fairfax area or to West Los Angeles. Harry's home was more modest than Ben's. His family consisted of his wife, Anna; daughter, Rose; and son, Albert, who was a dentist.

Harry invited me to stay the night; we spent the evening discussing my family and life in Israel.

The next morning, after breakfast, Harry took me on a tour of Twentieth Century Fox Studios, where he had access. I got to see how a movie was made. The experience was fascinating, because I had never dreamt of such a thing. I recalled my early encounters with movies in Israel, which consisted of climbing a tree to catch a glimpse of the screen at an open-air theater in Tel Aviv.

I needed a new living space to better suit my needs. I moved out of the Nidelmans' house and in with another family, who lived at 837 North Hudson Avenue. I realized I needed to find an additional job to help pay my rent and other expenses. As I mentioned, I had already found work at Congregation Knesseth Israel of Hollywood; on Saturday afternoons, I would be tutoring students for bar and bat mitzvah. I also secured a job teaching Hebrew on weekdays at Temple Emanuel, in Beverly Hills. (This work would lead to the formation of a Hebrew day camp that I led for several summers.)

In order to teach at a Hebrew school, however, one needed to be certified by the Bureau of Jewish Education (now known as Builders of Jewish Education—BJE) in Los Angeles. Upon reviewing my qualifications, they recommended that I take classes at the University of Judaism (now known as American Jewish University). Between studying at LACC during the day and at the University of Judaism at night, and working on weekends, my schedule was very full. Fortunately, the young women I dated were willing to meet me at 10:00 p.m.

Chapter 19

From Frog Legs to Vegetarian Pigeon: Professors and Roommates

MY FIRST COURSE at Los Angeles City College was in business. The instructor was very pleasant, and he took a special interest in me because I was an immigrant, like he was. We had many engaging conversations, some over lunch. One of the subjects he covered in class was the stock market. I was not familiar with this form of trading. He advised us to invest a small amount in a mutual fund, saying, "It will be your best investment and your worst." I found this insight to be accurate. I bought one hundred dollars of Massachusetts Investors Growth. It was a *poor* investment in the sense that, over sixty years later, I still own it, and it has not yielded much. It was a *good* investment in that it helped me realize there must be better things to do with my hard-earned money, prompting me to continue my pursuit of becoming an international entrepreneur.

One of my most enjoyable classes was French conversation. The instructor, Mr. Hirsch, had a wonderful sense of humor. Our final exam was highly unusual: We all went to a French restaurant on Sunset Boulevard, where

Summer camp, 1951. (I am in the second row from the back, seventh from the left.)

we had to use French to order the dishes he recommended. These included escargot (snails) and frog legs. Mr. Hirsch assured us that upon completion of the meal, we would receive an A in the class. Most of us had never heard of these "delicacies" much less eaten them. While some students thought the frog legs tasted like chicken, most of us couldn't stomach them. Mr. Hirsch took home a lot of leftovers, and we all got As.

In the summer of 1951, I worked again at the Jewish Community Center's day camp. After that ended, I kept my promise to visit my uncle Pesach and his family. I was joined by a friend from Israel who also wanted to go to New York. To be economical, we reserved a car that a rental company needed to relocate back to its originating office. The company covered the cost of gas and accommodations! Hoping to earn a bit of money, we advertised in the newspaper for other travelers to fill the empty seats in the car. We received several responses and selected a married couple and a single man to go with us. They each paid about sixty dollars for the ride, a reasonable rate.

We stopped overnight in Las Vegas—another "first" for me. In 1951, the famous Las Vegas Strip, located just south of the city limits, featured several motels and only a few hotels, such as the Hotel Last Frontier and El Rancho Vegas. Across the street from the El Rancho Vegas, a new hotel was being built: the Sahara. I couldn't know it at the time, but several years later, I would spend my honeymoon there. Other hotels in operation included the Flamingo, opened by mobster Bugsy Siegel in 1946; and the Desert Inn, where the Wynn stands today.

At the Sahara Hotel and Casino construction site, Las Vegas, August 1951

We stayed at one of the small motels on the Strip and ate at the Flamingo's buffet. The food was plentiful, excellent, and cheap. After dinner, we went downtown. I was dazzled by the glittering lights and neon signs. We played slot machines, which I found incredibly noisy, but didn't see a show; we had to return to the hotel and go to sleep, because we were driving the next morning.

On the way out of Vegas, the married couple got into a big argument. We asked them to stop fighting, since the commotion was making it hard to drive. But the verbal sparring increased. My friend angrily told the husband and wife that if they didn't end their bickering, he was going to drop them off on the side of the road. His threat had no effect, so he pulled over and forced them to get out. As he started to drive away, they ran after us. I asked my friend to stop the car. I got out and informed the couple that unless they ceased their quarreling, we would not let them back in. They stopped, and we finally had some peace.

Our next stop was Salt Lake City, Utah, where our passengers went to a hotel. My friend and I had heard there was a Jewish community in the city, which we confirmed. We attended the Shabbat service, after which a family invited us to have dinner with them and to stay overnight at their home rather than go to a hotel. They were very pleased to welcome us, as they had never met young people from Israel. My friend and I fielded a constant flow of questions about Israel, our schooling, and our future plans.

The next day, we collected our passengers at their hotel and continued on to Omaha, Nebraska. When we finally got there, we each enjoyed a huge steak.

Driving across the United States was a fascinating adventure. Everywhere we stopped, we experienced the beauty and majesty of the landscape. We were moved by the atmosphere of peace, and the friendship extended to us.

We arrived in New York about a week after we set off from Los Angeles. We left our passengers at their destinations. My friend dropped me off at my uncle's and returned the car to the rental company. When Uncle Pesach greeted me, I was surprised to find that his family wasn't there. He explained that they were "in the Catskills." I wondered what that meant. I found out the next day that the Catskill Mountains were a popular resort area in the state of New York, about 100 miles (160 kilometers) north of New York City. Families from the city commonly rented bungalows in the Catskills during the hot, muggy summer months. At the time, the top two hotels were the Concord and Grossinger's.

Catskills resorts catered primarily to Jewish people, serving superb kosher cuisine. These year-round hotels were situated next to small lakes that offered water sports, such as swimming and boating. Guests at Grossinger's could do laps in an Olympic-size outdoor swimming pool. Other activities included horseback riding, tennis, golf, and strolling on beautiful paths. Women played bridge and mah-jongg (a game using tiles with Chinese characters and symbols on them). Entertainment was provided in the evenings by the likes of comedians George Burns and Shecky Greene, singing quartet the Ames Brothers, crooner Eddie Fisher, and stand-up comic Michel Rosenberg—my cousin from Warsaw.

Uncle Pesach's family spent the summer at a bungalow village not far from the Concord. He worked as a typesetter

Eva, Jack, Sherry, and Pesach Duksin, 1957

during the week and came up on weekends. That weekend, I had the pleasure of accompanying him. I enjoyed seeing my little cousins. Jack was fascinated with cowboys and Indians, so I pretended to be a cowboy who had come all the way from the West Coast; he called me "partner." His younger sister, Sherry, was adorable.

While in the Catskills, I met my cousin Michel Rosenberg, whom I mentioned before. In addition to playing the Catskills, he acted in Yiddish theater in New York City and portrayed a character called Cousin Muttel on the 1950s television show *The Goldbergs*. His acting credits also included thirteen Yiddish films between 1931 and 1950. Michel's English-Yiddish comedy routines were recorded, including one called "Getzel Goes to a Baseball Game." He also entertained with Mickey Katz, an American musician and humorist.

After I watched Michel perform, he invited me to join him and some of the other actors and actresses for drinks. We had a great time telling jokes and funny stories. Michel got a little tipsy and tried to introduce me to some young ladies. He invited me to attend the next night's show, and I gladly accepted. I certainly enjoyed my time with him. In the early 1960s, Michel came to Los Angeles in a Mickey Katz production called "Hanukkah in Santa Monica," a musical comedy variety show.

My friend and I found another car from the rental company to drive back to Los Angeles but didn't take any passengers this time. In September, I resumed classes at Los Angeles City College and the University of Judaism, as well as my teaching and tutoring jobs. I graduated from LACC summa cum laude in February 1952. My professors were impressed with my work ethic and good grades, and I was nominated to become a member of Sigma Tau Sigma, the Department of Social Sciences Scholastic Honor Society. I felt a deep sense of gratitude to these professors, who opened the door for me to achieve my goal of becoming an instructor at the university level, a first in my family.

At the graduation ceremony, I was presented with a special award that qualified me to receive a scholarship from UCLA (which I was later granted). This prize was a tremendous honor—and a relief, because despite my work at the synagogues, my expenses (including rent and the constant repair of the Nash) prevented me from saving money and purchasing a more reliable car. Most importantly, I had accumulated more units toward qualifying for acceptance at UCLA.

I was later recognized by LACC at a special awards banquet in June. The main honoree was Cecil B. DeMille, the famous filmmaker. I was very excited to attend this ceremony because the awards were being presented by one of my favorite movie stars, Ginger Rogers. She gave me a hug, and a kiss on the cheek. That moment was very special to me because I admired her so much.

While waiting for the fall semester to begin at UCLA, where I would enter as a junior, I took a few business classes at California State University, Los Angeles.

Back in March, the Bureau of Jewish Education had granted me a pupil-teacher certificate, but I still needed to complete some courses at the University of Judaism. Dr. David Lieber was one of my teachers there; he would later serve as the school's president, from 1963 to 1992. The university was located at 612 South Ardmore Avenue, not far from where I lived. But the Nash was nearing the end of its usefulness, and I knew I was going to have to part with it. The first dealer I took it to had absolutely no interest in it. He told me, "Drive your clunker off the lot while it can still run." I approached another dealer.

"Sir, I would like to trade in my car for a new car, and then pay the rest."

"What kind of car do you have?" he asked.

"A 1939 Nash coupe," I said firmly.

"A Nash?" he wondered aloud. "I've never known anyone who had one. I didn't know they still existed!"

I walked him over to my car. He encouraged me look around the lot while he assessed it. "Prices are on the windows," he called out as I walked off. A four-year-old Plymouth caught my attention. It was marked $350. It looked clean and operable, so the dealer and I took it for a test drive. When we got back, he explained the warranty terms.

"I'm interested," I told him.

"While most dealers would probably pay you to take your Nash off their lot," he said, "I collect antique cars. And I know yours is rare. So I'll take it as a trade-in."

I was excited and relieved. "What's the price of the car now?"

"Factoring in your trade, $150," he said.

I paid him, signed some papers, and drove away happy. The Plymouth would serve me well for the next three years.

I then decided to see Jill. She was always refreshing company and up for having fun. Surprised to see my new car, she was pleased I had gotten rid of the Nash.

"Let's go for a ride," she suggested.

"Are you familiar with the UCLA campus?" I asked. "I'd like to take a tour of it. I'm hoping to go there in the fall."

To my surprise, there weren't any paved parking spaces at UCLA, only an open piece of land. First, we visited Royce Hall and Powell Library. I had never seen such an extensive collection of books before. We viewed the economics and law buildings, which were near each other, as well as the sports field. UCLA was probably ten times the size of LACC, but not nearly as big as it is now. Summer classes were in session, so we saw students walking on campus. The atmosphere was relaxed and enjoyable. When we returned to Jill's house, we snacked on cookies.

"Jill," I said, "the original family you recommended, the Nidelmans, were very kind, and I enjoyed living with them. I was fortunate to find another place to live on my own. But now I want to move closer to UCLA. Do you have any suggestions?"

"My dad knows a lot of people in the Jewish community," she replied. "I'll see if he can recommend a nice place for you close to campus."

In the summer, I returned to the Jewish Community Center's day camp, this time as head counselor of an age group. Part of my job was to interview people who wanted to become counselors; I was happy to recognize some of the applicants from my camping trip to Big Bear Lake two years earlier. I got to know my fellow counselors, who invited me to their homes and taught me more about Jewish life in LA. I also had the opportunity to visit new and exciting places with the children, such as the See's Candies factory, a Jewish center on Olympic Boulevard that had a swimming pool, the Los Angeles County Museum of Art (LACMA), and the La Brea Tar Pits (an Ice Age excavation site).

I wrote quite a few letters to my family, who were very pleased with my achievements at LACC and my scholarship to UCLA. They urged me to continue my studies.

Jill informed me about a family that was renting out a room. I visited them one evening, at 1232 South Alexandria Avenue. The couple was in their forties and had two children, a boy and a girl (ages seven and nine, respectively). We discussed the terms: $200 a month for room and board.

The husband gave me a tour of the house and backyard. The home was small but quaint, and in a nice area. I answered a few questions about my background and my studies, and they seemed pleased.

"Shami, you look like a nice young man," the husband began. "We would be glad to rent the room to you. Don't worry about our children. They are quiet and won't bother you."

I thought for a moment and then announced, "I would be happy to be your tenant! I'll be ready to move in next week."

At dinner the following day, I informed the family on North Hudson Avenue that I would be moving out. "Living here was like living with my own family," I told them. I had been accepted to the university by then, so I said, "As you know, I'm going to be studying at UCLA, which is a bit of a distance from here. It is with sadness that I leave your home and move closer to campus. All of you have been extremely kind to me, and I am so grateful to you. I have already made arrangements to leave at the end of the month."

I could see the disappointment on their faces. No one answered for several minutes.

The wife broke the silence. "Shami, you were like a part of our family. Both my husband and I will miss you. But you have made an important choice. All of us wish you the very best."

"My wife expressed my sentiments," the husband said. "If there is anything we can do to help you, please let us know."

I moved in with my new family. I took my meals with them, including on Sunday nights, when they went out to dinner at a delicatessen or a Chinese or Italian restaurant. Once we went to a kosher place on Fairfax Avenue. Every time, the wife ordered large portions, and there were always leftovers. She took these home in special bags she had brought with her, and we had variations on the leftovers for the rest of the week. Needless to say, she was quite frugal! My relationship with the family was warm and pleasant, so I didn't mind the recycled meals.

That summer, my new hostess took the children to visit her family in Chicago, leaving her husband and me to fend for ourselves. We went out to dinner to his favorite restaurants, occasionally even splurging on a steakhouse.

One July evening, he suggested we go to a strip joint, but I already had plans. So he went to bed, and I went out with my friends. I returned home late and went to sleep, only to be awakened at 4:52 a.m. by tremendous shaking and rattling in the house. When I got up later that morning, he was very angry. He shouted at me for having come home drunk with my friends and making a ruckus, moving furniture and breaking glasses. I tried to convince him that I wasn't responsible for the commotion or the damage. We soon heard on the radio that there had been a 7.3-magnitude earthquake in Kern County. It was the strongest quake in California since the one in San Francisco in 1906. Hardest hit was a town called Tehachapi, forty miles southeast of Bakersfield. When my host realized his mistake, he apologized and made me promise I wouldn't tell his wife he wanted to go to a strip joint—which we did two nights later.

In the fall of 1952, I entered UCLA as an economics major. I decided to move closer to the university. On campus,

I put my name on a list for people seeking roommates; I was lucky to find one. In December, he and I rented a place in Westwood, on Glendon Avenue.

My roommate, Wolfgang Busse, had received a scholarship from his church in Münster, Germany, to attend a school in Austin. A vegetarian, he found life in Texas—the top cattle state in the country—extremely difficult. With his parents' help, he moved to Los Angeles to study chemistry at UCLA. A shy man, Wolfgang loved to read poetry, especially Goethe and Schiller. On our first evening as roommates, he insisted on reading some poems to me in German. Because I knew Yiddish, at least some of it made sense. I chuckled to myself as I recalled my conversation with my brother in Tel Aviv, in which he encouraged me to explore the works of Goethe and Schiller. He was getting his wish!

Wolfgang and I took our meals with our hostesses, two former teachers who owned the house on Glendon. They didn't know about Wolfgang's vegetarian diet, so they served fish at our first meal. He was able to eat a baked potato and vegetables but volunteered to prepare dinner the next evening. The ladies accepted his offer, and we were all excited to see what he was going to serve. Imagine our surprise when we entered the dining room to find plates of potatoes and canned "ersatz" (imitation) meats that his parents had sent him. The smell of the items was so strong that it was almost unbearable.

"What is all this?" the ladies asked.

"The finest vegetarian substitutes for liver, chicken, turkey, pork—and best of all, pigeon," he answered.

"All this sounds very good," one lady said, "but I'm not very hungry." The second echoed her sentiments. They both left the room.

I didn't want to embarrass Wolfgang, so I tried the "turkey" and potato. It was like eating spoiled turnips. I asked him if he still had the cans, so he could put the food away and save it for the following day. Later that evening, when the ladies returned home from going out to eat, Wolfgang said he had another surprise for them.

"Another surprise?" one of them asked uneasily.

He proceeded to recite his favorite poem by Goethe, in German. Even though they didn't understand the language, the ladies listened courteously.

The next day, we found a note informing us that we could stay for the month for which we had already paid, but that we should look for other accommodations. And for the future, they would do the cooking, and no more "ersatz" food was allowed in the house.

Wolfgang was quite offended by their lack of appreciation for his efforts. I held back telling him that his meal was not so tasty, and his poetry not so enthralling. The stench of the canned foods had lingered, and I understood why we were being asked to leave.

Of course, Wolfgang and I were upset that we now had to spend our little free time looking for a new place to live. We combed the classifieds in UCLA's *Daily Bruin* and eventually found another house in Westwood.

I liked Wolfgang; he was considerate, kind, and pleasant to be with. I felt empathetic toward him because he was somewhat lost in the American lifestyle. In spite of his shyness, he loved to meet American women; he kept asking me to introduce him to my female friends. I decided to invite him to a picnic one Sunday afternoon at the Japanese garden at UCLA. Excited about the occasion, he came dressed in a suit and tie, even though the day was very warm. Wanting to impress the young women there, he brought along his book of Goethe and started to read poetry in German. He suggested that after lunch he read a poem by Schiller. Since he didn't have the book of Schiller with him, he left to retrieve it. While he was gone, the girls asked me, "Where did you find this guy? Who's Goethe? Who's Schiller? We don't understand a word of German!" They didn't want to meet him again. When he came back, they excused themselves.

After they had gone, Wolfgang mused, "What nice girls! It's a shame they didn't get to hear the delightful poetry of Schiller."

I kept to myself what they had said. And I never tried to play matchmaker again. (Clearly, I did not have my mother's skills at introducing possible romantic partners.) My friendship with Wolfgang continued through his graduation and return to Germany, where he taught and eventually attained a doctorate in chemistry.

At UCLA, I was fortunate to have some excellent instructors in the Economics Department. One of them had studied with Milton Friedman, a Nobel Prize winner in economics. He gave me a deep understanding of the conservative school of economics. I enjoyed interacting with my fellow students. Three of them became very good friends. We often had lunch together in the cafeteria at Kerckhoff Hall while we discussed economics and other courses we were taking. I was intrigued by stories of their lives before they came to UCLA. They were not from Los Angeles; in fact, they came from Illinois, North Dakota, and Montana. And they were keen to hear about my life in Israel. A few times, they tried to get me to eat a ham sandwich; I resisted, however, because Jewish dietary laws prohibit the consumption of pork.

My friend from North Dakota was an avid skier. He invited me to go skiing with him in his home state, but my work schedule didn't allow it. At the time, in the 1950s, my friend was interested in computer science; he was convinced that computers would come to play a significant role in American industry. Of course, he was correct! Upon graduation, he took a job at a bank and became involved in the early development of the high-tech aspects of business.

In addition to wonderful teachers and warm friendships, I enjoyed other aspects of my life at UCLA, including concerts, special lectures, and performances at Royce Hall. I especially liked my work as a teaching assistant in the Economics Department during my senior year. This job enabled me to develop friendships with the students, who were mostly freshmen and sophomores. Unfortunately, because I was so busy, these pleasant relationships were necessarily brief.

While I studied until ten o'clock most evenings, I still found time for a social life. One of the girls I met invited me to her sorority house. The attention of her "sisters" somewhat overwhelmed and embarrassed me. She asked me to a couple of dances and introduced me to her favorite drink: beer. It wasn't then, and still isn't, a beverage I enjoy.

The rabbi at Congregation Knesseth Israel of Hollywood, where I worked on weekends, made sure I met a few "nice Jewish girls." My experiences with them were mixed. I made a date with one young woman for dinner on a Saturday night. When I arrived at her home, which was near Westwood, her father greeted me. He invited me into their beautiful living room, where I sat with him and his wife while their daughter was "getting ready." They offered me a cup of tea and some cookies, and then proceeded to bombard me with questions. They asked where I lived, what I was studying, and if I was supported by my parents or already self-sufficient. When I told them my major, they asked if one could make a nice living in economics. Eventually, my date appeared, beautifully coiffed and dressed, and rescued me from this interrogation. We went on several dates, but I wasn't ready to get deeply involved.

In June 1954, I graduated from UCLA with a BA in economics. During the summer, I came up with the idea of having a Hebrew-speaking day camp for post–bar mitzvah boys at Temple Emanuel. Both the rabbi and the education director liked the concept very much, so I developed the camp. We went on field trips to places like the La Brea Tar Pits and the LA Times Building; the boys would then describe their experiences using the language skills they had learned in Hebrew school. The temple's youth director, Mr. Friedman, also wanted the boys to be exposed to other Jewish experiences, so we visited some live-away camps in the area, including Camp Alonim in Simi Valley and Camp Hess Kramer in Malibu. The boys were amazed at some of the religious traditions that were new to them.

Our most memorable excursion was to Camp Machaneh, an Orthodox boys' camp in Acton. We arrived at lunchtime, and the rabbi supplied us with kipot (skullcaps). We washed and said *Ha-motzi* (the blessing over the bread) and had a typical camp lunch, which consisted of tuna or egg salad sandwiches, cheese, milk, and fruit. Afterward, we followed along as the Machaneh boys chanted the *birkat hamazon* (blessing after the meal). We rested for an hour during the extreme heat of the day. Then the Machaneh boys challenged my campers to a game of soccer. All the boys at Machaneh wore an undergarment with four knotted tassels that stuck out beneath their shirts. These tassels, called tzitzit, are required attire for Orthodox Jewish males.

My boys were surprised and tickled by the sight of the tzitzit flying around each boy as he ran. The playing field was not grass but dirt; after all, the camp was in the Antelope Valley, at the western tip of the Mojave Desert. My boys enjoyed the game, even though they lost. Afterward, everyone appreciated the refreshing water of the man-made swimming hole. As the sun set, my campers asked about dinner. We were told that the Mincha (afternoon prayer service) and Maariv (evening prayer service) came first. When my campers grumbled, I told them, "When you are in Rome, you do as the Romans do, and when you are at Camp Machaneh, you do as they are doing."

We stayed overnight and awoke to the Shacharit (morning prayer service). My boys complained again but went along with it. After a really good kosher breakfast, we said our goodbyes and thanked Camp Machaneh for the unique experience.

At the end of the summer, I flew to New York to attend the wedding of my sister. Chana was working in New York as head nurse in the operating room at Montefiore Hospital. She was marrying Akiva Cohen, also an Israeli. I stayed with Uncle Pesach and his family. Three days before the wedding, I suffered an appendicitis attack and was rushed to Montefiore Hospital for surgery! Despite my doctor's advice to the contrary, I went to the wedding and even did some dancing.

Chana and Akiva remained in New York for a while and then returned to Israel. His work took them to Brussels, Belgium, for a few years and then back to Israel again.

Chapter 20

Hanukkah Cookies: Sweet Love

WHEN CLASSES AT UCLA started again in September, I was a graduate student studying for my MA in international economics. My economics professor, Dr. Gorter, was very demanding; his weekly seminars were tough. One evening, he invited the class to his modest home in Culver City, for tea and cookies. A dozen of us sat on the floor of Dr. Gorter's small living room, facing a roaring fire, as he lectured us on how the study of economics touches many aspects of life. Unlike in the classroom, he was rather friendly; he explained that he required intensive effort from us because he wanted us to be successful in our professions.

In the middle of December, we had a particularly difficult exam that ended at about nine o'clock at night. Exhausted, I decided to relax by attending a combined Christmas-and-Hanukkah party at the University Religious Conference building, just off campus. Looking around the room, I spotted a very attractive young woman with light brown hair. She didn't look Jewish, despite holding a tray of Hanukkah cookies. Intrigued, I approached her.

"My name is Sam Rimmon," I said. "What can you tell me about these cookies?" I recognized that they were shaped and decorated as Hanukkah symbols, but I wanted to know why this non-Jewish woman was serving Hanukkah cookies. Her name was Joan, and in a very pleasant voice, she told me the meaning of the symbols. Mishearing my last name as "Ramón," she thought I was from South America and not Jewish.

Taken by her lovely looks and friendly personality, I invited her for coffee. After the party was over, we drove to Zucky's Delicatessen in Santa Monica. Joan spent the rest of the evening explaining Hanukkah to me. She was not only Jewish but proud to be, and quite knowledgeable about Judaism. When I took her to her home on Arnaz Drive in Beverly Hills, where she lived with her parents, I confessed that I was not only Jewish but from Israel. Her face lit up. That was the moment she fell in love with me, I found out later. I asked her for another date, but it would have to wait until I returned from a counselor job over winter break at Camp Hess Kramer in Malibu.

When I got back, we had two dates, one to a movie and one to dinner. I fell in love. Because my intentions were serious, I invited her to see where I lived. I was renting a room in an apartment on Veteran Avenue that was owned by two elderly women. Both were pleasant, and one was completely blind. During that visit, I told Joan about my humble lifestyle and very limited financial resources. She seemed unconcerned. Her family was of modest means, and she was accustomed to living simply. She had dropped out of UCLA for various reasons just three weeks earlier, and she was working as a typist clerk in the acquisitions office of the Engineering Department. I saw no reason to wait. I proposed.

After Joan and I became engaged, the Solnit family invited us to a buffet luncheon at the Brentwood Country Club, where they were members. Joan's parents, Ruth and Leonard Glanz, and her teenage brother, Richard, were also there. A growing boy, Richard went back many times to refill his plate. I was quite impressed by his appetite!

We had settled on marrying in June, after school was over. But we were very much in love, so on March 17, 1955, during Joan's lunch hour, we went to city hall to get our license. We decided on the spot to get married by a judge. But we didn't want to miss having a Jewish ceremony, so we didn't tell anyone about the civil one. As it turned out, the

From left to right, Bertha Solnit (Ben's wife), Louis and Fanny Roth (friends of the Solnits), Yeshaiahu Rimmon (my father), and Ben Solnit (my cousin) in Israel, 1952

Janet (Joan's best friend), Leonard (Joan's father), Ruth (Joan's mother), Joan, myself, Chana (my sister), and Akiva (Chana's husband) at our wedding, 1955

wedding date we had chosen, June 19, was the same day as my graduation for my master's degree. Obviously, I chose to attend the wedding. We were married by Rabbi Bernard Harrison at Temple Emanuel in Beverly Hills. Our ceremony was one of the first in the temple's new building on Clark Drive. The reception took place at Joan's parents' house on Arnaz. We danced the hora in the backyard, accompanied by my harmonica.

Chana and Akiva came from New York for the wedding; Akiva was my best man. Joan's best friend from her youth in Detroit, Janet Katz, traveled from Stanford University to be her maid of honor. Ben and Bertha Solnit and their friends Louis and Fanny Roth also attended.

Joan had grown up in a family that did not keep Jewish traditions, but in the summer of 1954, she attended a camp for eighteen- to twenty-six-year-olds for learning and living a Jewish life. The camp was situated at Brandeis Camp Institute (BCI) in Santa Susana, California. Its name changed several times over the years and is now the Marilyn

Joan and I dancing at our wedding, 1955

and Sigi Ziering Brandeis Collegiate Institute in Brandeis, California. BCI was on the same site as Camp Alonim, where I brought my Hebrew day camp boys. It seems that Joan was at BCI at the same time I was at Camp Alonim with my boys, but, alas, we had to wait six months to meet.

The experience at BCI ignited Joan's passion for Judaism. She and I wanted to establish a traditional Jewish home. Though we did not keep strictly kosher, we avoided the foods forbidden under Jewish dietary laws. Therefore, we were very surprised by the main course my mother-in-law, Ruth, had planned for the reception: a baked ham! As I mentioned before, pork is not fit for consumption according to the Jewish religion. Despite our protestations, Ruth said it was what her friends enjoyed, and she was going to serve it. Joan and I didn't eat, and we soon drove off to Las Vegas for our honeymoon at the Sahara Hotel.

We had our first breakfast at Foxy's Delicatessen, where I tried to teach Joan how to play chess. By the end of our honeymoon, she could identify the pieces, but we never actually played a game. We had a wonderful week, dining at many hotels and going to late shows, where you could get in for a cup of coffee and a piece of cake. Since it was summer, we also spent some time by the pool.

A few months after our return, Joan left her job at UCLA and started working at a bank in Westwood. Until January, we lived in the room I had been renting from the older ladies as well as a second room across the hall, which another student had vacated. When Joan became pregnant, however, we needed more living space. We leased a side-by-side duplex on Westholme Avenue, just south of

Santa Monica Boulevard. It had one bedroom, a combined living-and-dining room, a small bathroom, and a kitchen. It was all we could afford, because Joan had to stop working as we awaited the birth of our child, and our main income was my salary as a teaching assistant at UCLA.

Shortly after our wedding, I began my efforts to attain American citizenship. I sought to become an American citizen for several reasons:

1. The United States is the finest and most beautiful country in which an immigrant could live.
2. The United States offered the best opportunity for me to realize my dream of becoming an entrepreneur.
3. The people of the United States are the kindest and most helpful.
4. I was overwhelmed by the concept of "Life, Liberty and the pursuit of Happiness," as mentioned in the U.S. Declaration of Independence.

Several years later, on May 29, 1959, I went downtown to the Federal Building and, along with many other immigrants, was sworn in as a United States citizen. I was delighted.

Chapter 21

Malaga Wine: Achieving My Dreams

I MADE EVERY EFFORT to improve our financial situation. At a New Year's Eve party, I sat with Joan and composed a letter to Mr. Le Conte, director of Rodier Fabrics in Paris; as you may recall, I had been the company's agent, through Green Brothers, in Palestine. I inquired if they would like a representative in California. To my pleasant surprise, I received a positive response. Mr. Le Conte came to Los Angeles, accompanied by his wife, to discuss the possibilities. We reminisced about their visit to Palestine many years earlier, when we dined and danced on a boat on the Yarkon River. Mr. Le Conte made me Rodier's West Coast representative. He provided me with samples of their line of woolen textiles.

One of our first meetings was with Jax of California, a Beverly Hills clothing designer. We invited their buyers to our home to view the collection. While Joan fed our new baby, Elana, in the kitchen, I presented the samples in the living room. Jax placed an order, and Joan and I were in the import business!

We wanted to diversify the commodities we were bringing into the United States, so I visited the local consulates of several countries. I discovered a potentially profitable item from Germany: a ballpoint pen that wrote with perfumed ink and had refills in different fragrances. The pens were attractive, with a plastic body that came in several colors and a gold filigree cover. We were very interested in getting exclusive rights to distribute the pen, at least in the western part of the United States.

I wrote a letter to the company requesting samples, for market research. I took the pens to UCLA and asked people who were passing on the quad what they thought of them and how much they would pay for them. I had a notebook and was writing in it with the pen to demonstrate the fragrance. I discovered great interest. Some of the students wanted to buy them right then and there. Next I visited specialty stores, with even more favorable feedback. The shop owners were quite excited because they had never seen such an item. They wanted to place orders. The price at which I offered to sell the pens to the stores would bring us a very nice profit.

The company was willing to give us exclusivity, but we had to buy at least three thousand pens. They were ninety-eight cents apiece, and we didn't have the money for such a purchase. So I went to Bank of America to apply for a loan. The manager asked me what kind of collateral I had.

"I have a product on which I will receive a very nice profit when I sell it," I replied.

The manager went to check my account. When he returned, he said, "You must be kidding! You want the bank to loan you $3,000 when your balance is barely three hundred?"

Taking him into my confidence, I showed him the pen and the results of my market research. He was very impressed and said he would provide the loan on two conditions.

"First, you must guarantee two years of your salary," he said. That meant my salary would go directly to the bank. At the time, I was earning $1,500 a year teaching Hebrew school and working as a teaching assistant at UCLA. "Second," he continued, "I need two pens with all the refills—one for my wife and one for my daughter."

Joan and I decided to sell the pens by mail, so we could do it at home. We rented a post-office box for receiving orders and placed an ad in the Sunday magazine of the *Los Angeles Times*. The ad ran the Sunday after Thanksgiving, and on Monday, I checked the box; to my great disappointment, it was empty. On Tuesday, the only item in the box was a bill for *renting* the box. On Wednesday, in a panic, I opened the box to find another notice from the postmaster. Thinking it was for the customs on a package of pens I was expecting, I was deeply worried; I didn't have the money to pay the duties.

When I went to the postmaster, he asked, "Why did you get such a small box?" He handed me a huge canvas sack, filled with hundreds of envelopes.

I ran home, and Joan and I opened the bag. Tears filled our eyes when we saw all the orders and checks. Our success, however, was short-lived. About a month later, we received multiple requests for refunds because the pens were drying out. We contacted the company, and they explained that the alcohol in the perfume was causing the ink to evaporate. They reimbursed us for the damages.

Another product we tried to import and sell was French mustard, in tubes. Despite the handiness of the packaging, the American market was unreceptive. The item was a failure for us.

I was also in touch with Volvo, the car manufacturer. I had the opportunity to become the company's representative in California. However, the initial financial investment and the fact that I would have to give up my other ventures discouraged me from pursuing this option. Looking back, I regret not seeking the financial assistance that would have enabled me to participate in what has become such a successful enterprise.

We also investigated the sewing machine business, importing a sample machine that Joan used for many years.

Joan and I concentrated on the "schmatta" (garment) business. After representing Rodier successfully, we became agents for several manufacturers of natural-fiber fabrics in Italy, Switzerland, Germany, and England. We started attending international textile trade shows in Italy and Germany. During these trips to Europe, we also visited many manufacturers and purchased goods on our own.

Since our office was in our home, we used the services of a company that offered a mailing address; based on that address, our office appeared to be near Wilshire Boulevard and La Brea Avenue, about twenty miles (thirty-two kilometers) from where we lived in the San Fernando Valley. One year, a representative from a German velvet manufacturer wanted to visit us. He was staying at a hotel downtown and thought he could just walk over to our office. He didn't realize how sprawling Los Angeles is! He finally called us, and I went to meet him. We later visited customers in San Francisco together.

As Joan and I acquired more and more customers, I found myself working from early in the morning until late at night. We employed high school girls to assist us in secretarial jobs. When the goods arrived in Los Angeles, I would go to the airport (LAX) or to the port in San Pedro Bay, pay the customs duties, and deliver the goods to our local customers. For customers outside of Los Angeles, we would ship items via UPS.

Our four youngest children (from left to right, Dan, Adina, Ron, and Alissa) in front of the family store on Ventura Boulevard in Tarzana, California, 1966

Our office was a bedroom in our three-bedroom home in Reseda, for which we had paid $14,000. By 1960, our family had grown to include three children (Elana, Ron, and Adina), with a fourth on the way. We needed a bigger place, so we purchased a four-bedroom house in nearby Northridge, for $26,000. There, our office occupied a bedroom as well as part of the garage. Dan was born just two weeks before the move; Alissa came along in 1962.

Around 1964, we opened a retail store in Tarzana in partnership with another fabric businessman. The shop was called World of . . . Elegance. Our inventory consisted mainly of the goods we purchased in Europe. We also carried patterns and notions (such as buttons, thread, and ribbons). Our primary income, however, was from our wholesale business. And since we were planning to move from Northridge to West Los Angeles, we closed the store in 1967.

In January 1968, we relocated to a modest section of Bel Air, an affluent neighborhood west of Downtown Los Angeles. We joined Sinai Temple, a large Conservative synagogue, where our children attended Hebrew school and had their bar and bat mitzvahs. The bedrooms in our four-bedroom home accommodated just beds this time, with a den serving as our office. We remodeled the garage into a warehouse.

Our business grew in another way: we began to sell wholesale not just to designers and manufacturers but to retail fabric stores. Joan and I traveled to various cities, securing many new venues for our goods. We stayed in small motels and ate cheese and rolls on the road between customers. Many of our buyers became friends, and our sons still work with them today.

In 1971, U.S. Secretary of State Henry Kissinger made two trips to the People's Republic of China, paving the way for improved relations between the two countries. The following year, President Richard Nixon made his historic visit to China, resulting in the opening of trade between China and the United States. Shortly after, Joan and I attended a textile trade show in Frankfurt, Germany. There, in a very small room, we met two Chinese representatives wearing Mao suits (tunic-style suits named for Mao Zedong, founding father of the People's Republic of China). A German woman who spoke Chinese served as their interpreter. We were very interested in purchasing silk, the main source of which was China. We knew that the price of silk from China was considerably lower than what we were paying in Switzerland, France, Italy, and Germany. The agents were at the show just to survey the market, however, and didn't have any samples. They took our contact information to keep in touch.

When we returned to the trade show the next year, we met the Chinese reps again. To our amazement, they were no longer dressed in Mao suits but in Western-type suits, probably from the 1920s. A young Chinese woman who spoke English accompanied them, and they had silk samples with them this time. Their prices were incredibly low. We wanted to place an order, but they suggested we visit their factory in Suzhou, China, which we eventually did in 1984.

Much later, in 1977, as a sideline, we started importing a jam produced by the Israeli company 778. It was quite a good seller. In fact, the jam is found on shelves in many kosher markets today, imported by another company.

In 1984, Joan and I finally traveled to China. We flew from Los Angeles to Shanghai and took a train from Shanghai to Suzhou, arriving at around 11:00 a.m. We hired a taxi to take us to the factory and then wait to take us back to the train, which was leaving for Shanghai at 4:00 p.m. When we arrived at the factory, we were greeted by two people who didn't speak English. They got a third gentleman to converse with us. Offering us bitter tea, they inquired about the recent Olympics in Los Angeles. They were especially interested in photos Joan had taken with China's women's volleyball team when she volunteered during the games.

The English-speaking gentleman gave us a tour of the area where the silk was being extracted from silkworm cocoons. As we entered, the stench from the boiling cocoons was overpowering. "How do they stand it?" we thought. About a hundred women labored over steaming pots, pulling silk threads from the cocoons. They worked about ten hours a day.

Then he took us to see some silk fabrics. We selected about ten designs and were ready to buy them. But because we had traveler's checks, the sale required approval from Beijing. We were offered more tea as we waited.

"You are the first American businesspeople to purchase silks from us," the interpreter told us.

We were getting anxious, because we had to catch the train back to Shanghai. Several workers started measuring the fabric so we could take it with us. When the deal was completed, after over an hour, we ran out to the taxi. We arrived at the train just in time to board. The driver was shoving bags of fabric to us through the window of the moving locomotive! And we were on our way back to Shanghai.

Shanghai was a fascinating city. Except for the Bund (the riverfront boardwalk in central Shanghai), with its high-rises constructed during the early twentieth century, most of the buildings were old and shabby. There were hundreds of people in the streets, dressed in Mao suits. They were very curious about us, lifting their children up on their shoulders to get a look.

We also traveled all over Switzerland, by car, with Zurich as our base. We found the delightful Hotel Sonnenberg atop a mountain in Zurich. Family owned, it had a small zoo! The dining room offered a panoramic view of the city and Lake Zurich below. The breakfasts were great, and we developed a nice relationship with the owners. We were guests there many years in a row.

One time, we stayed in St. Gallen, about fifty miles (eighty kilometers) east of Zurich. The hotel had a swimming pool with a special effect: a machine that created waves! After taking a swim, I went into the steam room. All of a sudden, I heard people yelling, *"Es ist nicht getan"* ("It is not done"). I finally realized it was a *nude* steam room, so I took off my bathing suit. When I exited, I put my suit back on. Then I went into a room with a hot tub. But it was also a nude room. Somewhat embarrassed, I went back to our room.

Joan and I purchased a lot of textiles in Switzerland, mostly magnificent embroideries and beautifully printed cottons and silks. We became friends with several export managers and had interesting conversations with them about economics, trade, and world events. We even spent some time with their families.

The atmosphere of Switzerland was very peaceful, as the nation had not been involved in a war since 1847. The place was exceedingly clean. We saw people tidying their yards and the streets in front of their homes. The street-cleaning machines even worked in the rain.

We bought silks with exquisite designs in Como, the center of the Italian silk industry. They were very expensive, but we had a high demand for them from the designers we worked with in California. In Como, we had very nice relationships with the owners of the silk mills; among them was Mr. Giulio. He was very flamboyant, and one evening he called us to join him at Villa d'Este, a luxury hotel on Lake Como. Joan had a stomach virus and couldn't go, but Mr. Giulio convinced me to accept his invitation. He picked me up in his Cadillac, which could barely fit through the city's narrow streets. He tooted his unique horn, which played loud music.

"Why do you play your horn so late at night?" I asked him. "Aren't most people asleep?"

"This is how I call my friends to have a drink with me at the villa," he replied. Momentarily, two beautiful young women came out to the street. The four of us had drinks at Villa d'Este.

On a Sunday afternoon, Joan and I took a boat trip on Lake Como with Mr. Giulio and his wife and daughters. The vessel was large and filled with tourists. We cruised the lake, taking in beautiful vistas; the verdant hillsides and elegant houses were reflected in the water. When the boat stopped in Bellagio, we all got off and took a funicular up the side of the mountain; the view of the lake and the small towns along its banks was spectacular.

While visiting factories and showrooms in Germany, we took a side trip to Münster, to see my old college roommate, Wolfgang. Still a vegetarian, he was married and had one small son. He lived a very peaceful life, teaching chemistry at the University of Münster in the mornings and sitting in a coffee shop, reading the newspaper and discussing world events with his friends, in the afternoons. He spent evenings at home with his family. Wolfgang took us up in the mountains of Münster to see some very old villages. Then he showed us the detention camp where he had stayed as a boy. His mother was Jewish, and she was married to a non-Jew. During World War II, she and Wolfgang were interned with others who were in mixed

From left to right, Wolfgang and his son, Thomas; Joan; myself; and Wolfgang's wife, Carla, in Münster, Germany, 1959

Jewish/non-Jewish families. They were very lucky to have survived the Holocaust.

Joan and I annually attended a week-long trade show in Frankfurt, the one where we met the Chinese representatives. Every day, we went to the Messe, the grounds where the show was being held. We spent many hours walking the exhibition, to do research and meet new suppliers. In the evenings, we would find a restaurant that served *spargel*, white asparagus. This delicacy came into season in the spring. We encountered many preparations of *spargel*, but the one we loved most was steamed, with Hollandaise sauce.

One evening, we ordered ice cream for dessert, with the intention of sharing it. When the waiter brought it to the table, we asked for a second spoon. This request caused quite a stir. The other diners were taken aback to see us eating from one dish with *zwei löffel* ("two spoons"). A couple at the next table started a conversation with us about this apparently uncommon practice—and thus began a long friendship with Elke and Helmut. We would get together with them every year.

During the trade show in Frankfurt, hotel rooms were in short supply. One year, Joan and I didn't have a reservation, so the accommodations clerk at the Messe set us up in a place along the Main River. The room was very nice. It had a sink, but the toilet was down the hall. And there was no shower. The only bathtub was in a small alcove between the kitchen and the dining room, just across from the front entrance. This unusual tub was like a chair surrounded by porcelain. I found out it was used to wash the dishes! A fräulein filled the tub with hot water for me, and I got in.

She then proceeded to use the passageway to serve meals while I was soaking there! A freezing wind came in through the open front door, but the young woman didn't heed my requests to close it. She just smiled at me every time she passed. Needless to say, it was the last bath I took there.

At another hotel, the bathroom was so small that when I bent forward to shave my face, my bottom stuck out the door! In yet another hotel, the bathroom was a prefabricated unit that consisted of a sink, toilet, and shower inserted into a closet space. Occasionally, we were fortunate enough to stay at the luxurious InterContinental.

Traveling from country to country to select fabrics and bargain for satisfactory prices was hard work. It involved air, train, and car travel, as well as knowledge of multiple currencies. We tried to make these trips more enjoyable by developing friendships with manufacturers and sightseeing occasionally.

In England, we met a lovely Jewish couple who sold us woolens. Kuba and Rose lived in Golders Green, an area of London known for its large Jewish population. We spent several Saturday afternoons with them, walking in a beautifully landscaped park and talking about life in the Jewish community of London. Originally from Warsaw, Kuba was an avid stamp collector, as I had been in my youth. One weekend, we went with Kuba and Rose to Bournemouth, a resort town on the south coast of England. Our friendship with them lasted many years. They hosted some of our children when they traveled to London, and their daughter and her husband visited us in Los Angeles.

During our trips to France, we bought velvet, silks, embroideries, and woolen scarves. We always sought out the least expensive places to stay, to save our limited funds. At one hotel in Paris, the elevator accommodated two people at the most. Our luggage had to be sent up separately! The room was very small, and when we lay down on the bed, we sank into the mattress. Joan and I enjoyed visiting the city's famous landmarks, including the Eiffel Tower, Arc de Triomphe, and Notre Dame.

In Paris, as in other cities, we made friends with some of our business contacts. One gentleman, Mr. Lefebvre, was particularly helpful in guiding us to interesting places, such as the Left Bank, the Louvre, and the Jewish quarter. One night, he and his wife and children invited us to a kosher restaurant on the Champs-Élysées. A very sweet Malaga wine was served with dinner, and Joan thought it was delicious. She drank so much of it that when we left the restaurant, we had to hold her up!

Joan and I reciprocated Mr. Lefebvre's hospitality when he later came to Los Angeles. We invited him to dinner at a kosher restaurant on Fairfax called Tel Aviv. It served some unusual Jewish dishes, such as lungen (cow's lung) stew. We had eaten there quite often with our children, who were with us that night. Unbeknownst to us, our younger son, Dan, had thoughtfully brought along a can of air freshener to mask the stench in the smelly men's room, should our guest need to use it. We maintained our friendship and business relationship with Mr. Lefebvre for many years, just as we did with Kuba and Rose in London.

Our business trips extended to India. We bought silks, cottons, and saris in Bombay, Madras, and Cochin (now called Mumbai, Chennai, and Kochi, respectively).

At the time, visiting Bombay, on the west coast of India, was an unpleasant experience. We stayed at a Holiday Inn outside of Bombay and took a taxi into the city. Masses of people, as well as wandering cows, obstructed the streets. The inhabitants of Bombay led unhappy lives of extreme poverty. Parents taught their children to beg, sometimes maiming them to appear more pathetic.

We also saw many poor people in Madras, on the southeast coast of India. When we crossed over a creek, the stench was unbearable, as the water was polluted with sewage. You may be familiar with madras, the lightweight cotton fabric named after the city. Typically, this material features a multicolored design in plaid or stripes.

Joan and I found Cochin, in southern India, a much more pleasant place to conduct business. At one time, it was the center of India's Jewish population. We didn't witness the acute poverty there that we did in Bombay and Madras. We were amazed at the selection of saris offered to us; the colors and designs were so beautiful that we could not resist acquiring several. We also visited Paradesi Synagogue, the only synagogue still in use in the Jewish quarter of Old Cochin. Built in 1567, it was very striking, with flooring of blue-and-white Delft tile (made in the Netherlands in the sixteenth century).

In Bali, Indonesia, we purchased the island's specialty: batik cottons. The people making the batiks did it at home, where we called on them. Hand-dyeing batik fabrics with fine patterns remains a labor-intensive process.

Our trips to these diverse places were fascinating learning experiences. Among the many items we imported were woolen scarves from France, silk scarves from Italy, beautiful embroideries from Switzerland, cottons from Israel and Guatemala, stuffed toy llamas and llama wool from Peru, small carved wooden animals from Kenya, leather goods from Brazil, silk pillow covers from Thailand, and knitted dolls from New Zealand. Joan and I discovered that despite the differences between countries and cultures, you can develop friendships if you deal with people pleasantly and kindly.

Many years before the rise of the global economy, I had accomplished my dream of becoming an international entrepreneur. My goal to establish business and personal relationships around the world started with my import work as a teenager at Green Brothers in Tel Aviv. S. Rimmon & Co., Inc., is our legacy for three of our children—Ron, Adina, and Dan. We have transferred the company to them.

Through my real estate dealings, I was able to achieve my *second* life's dream, to provide my family with enough income to lead a comfortable life during my retirement. While I was still a young boy, my father had hoped to buy a tiny piece of land outside of Petach Tikvah. I accompanied him as he set out to make this purchase. He was eager and excited to own property where our family could live and set down roots. When my father was told he could not afford it, I saw his devastation. I felt his deep sadness and disappointment. At that moment, I became determined to acquire some real estate myself.

Having children of my own intensified my desire to own property. In 1963, with some of the funds we had accumulated from the business, we purchased a small commercial building with three storefronts in Granada Hills, a neighborhood adjacent to Northridge. We paid $40,000 for it, putting down $13,000 and carrying a mortgage. Two businesses leased space in the building; later, one business rented the whole thing. Eventually, we sold the property to buy another.

Later on, I took Joan and the children to look at some larger pieces of land north of Los Angeles and west of the San Fernando Valley, where there was great potential for growth and development. We negotiated a very reasonable price for a twenty-seven-acre parcel in a small community called Agua Dulce. The property was close to the Vasquez Rocks, where many Hollywood movies have been filmed, including *Blazing Saddles* (1974), *The Flintstones* (1994), *Planet of the Apes* (2001), and *Star Trek* (2009). The land was situated on a highway on a rising slope, with several acres zoned for commercial use. Just down the road was a small airport for private planes. There was a well on the property, along with a small house that provided a beautiful view of the area. We eventually sold the acreage for a handsome profit.

I realized my *third* life's dream, to share my experiences with others who could benefit from them, in 1980. I started teaching my first class in international trade (importing and exporting) at Los Angeles Valley College, in the San Fernando Valley. To my surprise, the room was overflowing! More than forty students wanted to take the class, exceeding the maximum enrollment, so some had to wait until it was offered again.

I had the same experience the next semester, at California State University, Northridge (CSUN). There, the more than sixty students who signed up were able to be accommodated.

In 1987, I published a book entitled *Importing: Your Guide to Fortune and Fulfillment*. This volume was—and still is—used as a text in my classes. I published a second edition in 2004 with chapters added to cover such subjects as Internet sales and some changes in the trade policies of the United States. The book emphasizes that international trade is not only financially rewarding but also extremely enjoyable.

I taught at CSUN for several years. In 1991, I was honored with an award for excellence in teaching. There was no monetary compensation associated with this award, but receiving it gave me a good feeling—that I was truly helping students who were seeking careers in this important field.

Published in 1987, my book on importing is used as a text in my classes

Eventually, I would teach at numerous other institutions, including Beverly Hills Adult School, Santa Monica College, Loyola Marymount University, West Los Angeles College, Pasadena City College, and Glendale Community College in the Los Angeles area; and the College of Southern Nevada and the University of Nevada, Las Vegas, in the Las Vegas area.

The classes were offered as a series of three sessions

plus an additional session in assertive business communication and negotiation—essential skills in international business and salesmanship.

Although my remuneration for teaching has been very modest, I am extremely gratified to be able to pass along what I have learned to my students. Based on their testimonials in my book on importing, I am deeply humbled to say I have been successful in helping them become international entrepreneurs. Moreover, I have benefitted from getting to know my students—their cultures, goals, and dreams.

Epilogue

DURING MY YEARS IN ZHABINKA, on Shabbat, my grandfather and I would study the Bible. I vividly remember reading the story of the Israelite hero Samson, whose exploits are described in the book of Judges. One day, Samson was walking on the road to Timnah with his mother and father. As they approached the vineyards of Timnah, a young lion came roaring toward Samson. The Spirit of the Lord made Samson so strong that he tore the lion apart with his bare hands. When Samson returned to Timnah several days later, he found the lion's carcass filled with a swarm of bees and some honey. Samson then challenged the young men of Timnah to solve a riddle based on his experience. Part of the riddle was, *"Me'az yatza matok"* ("From the bitter came something sweet").

This story made a deep impression on me and gave me hope that I could overcome the difficulties of my past and achieve my goals.

My youth was extremely hard. At times, I suffered from hunger, neglect, and loneliness. I was driven not only to surmount my situation but to accomplish much more. My decision to travel to America, in order to pursue my education, was heartrending. Leaving my parents, siblings, other relatives, and friends behind was emotionally very tough.

Creating my new life took a great deal of effort, patience, and adjustment. Because I lacked money and the

Celebrating my 93RD birthday with my family, December 2015

support of my family, a job was imperative, and the friendships I made were precious. Eventually, I was fortunate to be blessed with a loving and caring wife and children, who enabled and assisted me to reach my goals.

In the twilight of my life, I am very grateful to God for all that He has granted me. Soon, with His blessing, I will celebrate my ninety-fourth birthday. In spite of my age and the limitations it places on me, I fervently desire to continue my activities, which include helping my family, spending time with my friends, and giving seminars on international business. I feel it is my obligation to share with others my life's philosophy, which is based on my many years of experience.

What I Believe

I BELIEVE THAT GOD GRANTED US LIFE so we can make a contribution in the world, in any way we are able to do so. We ought to be grateful for the gift of life.

I believe that everyone can make a contribution. One way is to be supportive, kind, considerate, and compassionate to the people around you—your family, friends, and others in need. I believe that we should make an effort to enhance the quality of life not only for ourselves but for others, as well. We can do so by greeting every person we meet with a smile, and by having an open mind and an attentive ear. When a person needs your advice, share your knowledge and wisdom. When a person is feeling down, try to lift his or her spirits.

Another way to make a contribution is through work. I believe in the work ethic. I know from my own experience that hard work leads to fulfillment. You should pursue a profession that will enable you to be productive, self-sufficient, and content.

I believe that you should establish a list of priorities and goals, and make every effort to achieve them—even when circumstances become difficult and you face criticism.

The top priority is to maintain your health, to the best of your ability. Caring for your own physical well-being is important not just for you but for your family, so you can avoid becoming a burden on them.

You should also be an eternal student, not only in school but in life. Take lessons from your own experiences and those of others. During my many years of teaching college, I realized I could learn a great deal from my students, especially because they came from many different countries and cultures. My extensive dealings in international business allowed me to learn from my associates around the world, as well.

In concluding my book, I want to address a subject that is very close to my heart—the precious emotion of love. Poets, authors, playwrights, and songwriters have written widely about love. To me, it is a very personal, heartwarming feeling. I express my love to the Almighty in the daily prayer, "You shall love the Lord your God with all your heart, with all your soul, and with all your might." I have a deep love for my dear late parents, Rachel and Yeshaiahu; my dear late brother, Avraham; and my dear sister, Chana, who is living in Israel. The love I feel for my wife, children, grandchildren, and the rest of my family similarly knows no bounds. I love my friends and the many people with whom I have had relationships during my studies, in my business, and in my teaching. My love also extends to nature.

To me, love is the most beautiful and wonderful emotion with which humans are blessed. As expressed in the popular song from the 1950s, love is indeed a "many-splendored thing." To love and be loved is the pinnacle of human experience. It is the major source of joy, resulting in pure happiness—the moment when all doubt and tension are gone, and you feel at one with the universe.

Love enhances self-esteem. It is the best prescription for good health and peace. It provides a source of security and helps you reach your highest potential.

When you have love, "Every day is a kiss from above from the Angel of Love." It is within your power—and is indeed your obligation—to provide the experience of love to members of your family, your friends, and everyone around you. It is the best way to better your life and to improve the world.

Glossary

ABA. Hebrew for "father."

BAR MITZVAH. Hebrew for "son of the commandment." A bar mitzvah is a male child who, at the age of thirteen, becomes obligated to observe the commandments of Judaism. More commonly, the term is used to refer to the coming-of-age ceremony that commemorates this rite of passage. A girl celebrates a Bat Mitzvah, "daughter of the commandment."

BIRKAT HAMAZON. The blessing said after meals.

B'NAI B'RITH. The oldest Jewish service organization in the world. The name means "Children of the Covenant."

BRITISH MANDATE OF PALESTINE. A geopolitical entity in Palestine, administered by the British from 1920 to 1948, that served, in part, as a national home for the Jewish people.

CANTOR. The person who leads the congregation in melodic prayers during Jewish religious services.

CHALLAH. A twisted egg bread eaten on the Jewish Sabbath and holidays.

CHALUTZ. Hebrew for "pioneer." A chalutz was an immigrant to Palestine who helped develop agricultural settlements.

CHAMETZ. Bread, cake, or crackers containing a leavening agent, such as yeast; forbidden for use and consumption during Passover.

CHEDER. An elementary Jewish school in which children are taught Hebrew and Jewish studies. The Hebrew word cheder means "room," and the cheder is usually a small room attached to the synagogue.

CHOLENT. A heavy stew made of meat, beans, and vegetables that was cooked slowly overnight to be ready for a meal on the Sabbath afternoon.

CONCHIK. A switch or thin leather strap used to punish a disobedient child.

DIASPORA. The movement, migration, or scattering of a people away from an established or ancestral homeland.

DUNAM. A measure of land area, equal to approximately a quarter of an acre.

EFFENDI. A wealthy Arab absentee landowner.

EMA. Hebrew for "mother."

ERETZ YISRAEL. Hebrew for "the Land of Israel."

ERSATZ. Serving as a substitute, synthetic, or artificial, such as with "coffee" made from grain, or "meat" made from vegetarian ingredients.

FIER KASHES. The "four questions" traditionally asked by the youngest child at a Passover seder.

GABBAI. An assistant in a synagogue, often in charge of running the religious services.

GEFILTE FISH. A dish consisting of a seasoned, minced-fish mixture that is either stuffed inside a fish skin and cooked, or formed into patties and boiled in fish stock.

GENTILE. A non-Jewish person.

GROSCHEN. A former Polish monetary unit.

GYMNASIUM EREV. Hebrew for "night school."

HADAR OCHEL. Hebrew for "dining hall."

HAGANAH. A paramilitary organization founded in Palestine in 1920 to protect Jewish farms, kibbutzim, and residents. The Haganah later formed the basis for the Israel Defense Forces.

HAGGADAH. The printed text which sets forth the order of the Passover seder and tells the story of the Israelites' escape to freedom.

HA-MOTZI. The blessing said before eating bread.

HANUKKAH. A Jewish holiday lasting eight days, celebrated in November or December. The menorah (branched candle-holder) is lit each night of the festival.

HASHOMER HATZAIR. Hebrew for "The Youth Guard." This socialist movement, which started before Israel became a state, focused on protecting the rights of young workers.

"HATIKVAH." The Israeli national anthem. Hatikvah is Hebrew for *"The Hope."*

HAVDALAH. The Jewish ceremony marking the end of the Sabbath.

HIGH HOLIDAYS. The Jewish festivals of Rosh Hashanah and Yom Kippur.

HISTADRUT. An Israeli labor union founded in 1920.

HORA. A traditional Israeli circle dance.

ISRAEL DEFENSE FORCES (IDF). The armed forces of the State of Israel, founded in 1948.

KAPOTE. A black, satin, robe-like coat with a sash, worn by men on the Sabbath.

KIBBUTZ. A collective community in Israel that was traditionally based on agriculture. Today, kibbutzim (plural for kibbutz) are involved in many other sectors of the economy, including industrial manufacturing and the high-tech industry.

KIPAH. The small round cap worn by Jewish men, especially during prayer or religious study; also called "yarmulke." The plural of kipah is kipot.

KOSHER. Suitable or permitted to be consumed according to Jewish dietary laws.
KRAKOWIAK. A Polish dance similar to a Polka.
KUPAT CHOLIM. An Israeli health insurance program founded in 1911.
LA-AZAZEL. Hebrew for "to hell."
LAILA TOV. Hebrew for "good night."
LIRA. Former Israeli currency.
LULAV. A ritual item composed of palm, myrtle, and willow leaves used during the Jewish holiday of Sukkot (plural, lulavim).
MAARIV. Evening prayers.
MASHGIACH. A person who oversees the preparation of food according to kashrut (Jewish dietary laws).
MATZAH. Unleavened bread eaten at Passover.
MELAMED. Hebrew for "teacher," referring to a teacher in a cheder or other Jewish school.
MIKVAH. A ritual bath house.
MINCHA. Afternoon prayers.
MINYAN. A quorum required for prayer in Judaism.
MISHLOACH MANOT. Holiday gift basket of foods given on Purim.
MOHEL. A person who performs ritual Jewish circumcisions, usually a rabbi.
MOSHAV. An Israeli cooperative community consisting of individually owned farms that market their produce communally.
PARDES. Hebrew for "orchard."
PASSOVER. A Jewish holiday that commemorates the Exodus from Egypt; also called Pesach.
PONCHKE. A jelly donut.

PRUTAH. A former Israeli coin with the value of a penny (plural, prutot).
PURIM. A Jewish holiday commemorating Queen Esther's saving of the Jews of Persia from a death plot.
ROSH HASHANAH. The Jewish New Year, and the beginning of a ten-day period of introspection.
SCHLEP. Yiddish for "to pull" or "to drag."
SCHMATTA. Yiddish for "rag" but can refer to a garment or low-quality merchandise.
SCHTICK. A prank or comedic gimmick.
SEDER. A religious service and dinner that take place on the first two nights of Passover (on just the first night in Israel). The plural of seder is sedarim.
SHABBAT. Hebrew for "Sabbath." Shabbat is the seventh day of the week, Saturday, a day of rest and religious observance among Jews (plural, Shabbatot).
SHACHARIT. Morning prayers.
SHALOM. Hebrew for "peace." The word shalom is used as a greeting or farewell.
SHTETL. A small town with a large Jewish population. Shtetls existed in Central and Eastern Europe until the 1940s.
SHTIEBEL. A very small building or room used for Jewish worship.
SHTREIMEL. A large fur hat worn by religious men on Shabbat and Jewish holidays.
SUKKOT. The fall holiday commemorating the forty years that the Hebrews wandered in the desert following the Exodus from Egypt. Sukkot shaped the customs of the American holiday of Thanksgiving.
TALMUD. The authoritative text on Jewish law and tradition.

TARBUT. A network of secular schools in Europe in which the language of instruction was Hebrew. Tarbut schools existed primarily between the two world wars, in Poland, Romania, and Lithuania. The Hebrew word tarbut means "culture."

TEVET. The tenth month of the twelve-month Jewish calendar.

TODA RABA. Hebrew for "thank you very much."

TORAH. The five books of Moses, part of the Holy Scriptures.

TZITZIT. The fringes or tassels worn on the corners of a Jewish prayer shawl.

YESHIVA. A school of higher Jewish learning (plural, yeshivot).

YOM KIPPUR. The Day of Atonement, which concludes a ten-day period of introspection.

ZIONISM. A Jewish nationalist movement that arose in the late nineteenth century and that sought to reestablish a Jewish homeland in Palestine.

ZIONIST. An adherent of Zionism and supporter of Jewish nationalist identity. See Zionism.

CPSIA information can be obtained
at www.ICGtesting.com
Printed in the USA
FSOW01n1544030617
34718FS